Wild Harvest in the Heartland

Ethnobotany in Missouri's Little Dixie

Justin M. Nolan

UNIVERSITY PRESS OF AMERICA,® INC.
Lanham • Boulder • New York • Toronto • Plymouth, UK

Copyright © 2007 by
University Press of America,® Inc.
4501 Forbes Boulevard
Suite 200
Lanham, Maryland 20706
UPA Acquisitions Department (301) 459-3366

Estover Road
Plymouth PL6 7PY
United Kingdom

Library of Congress Control Number: 2006938973
ISBN-13: 978-0-7618-3653-7 (paperback : alk. paper)

Table of Contents

Preface

Ethnobotany, the study of the interrelations between people and plants, has come a long way since its inception a century ago. No longer associated with remote and exotic locales, ethnobotany has expanded into a household name. Equal parts anthropology and botany, ethnobotany is holistic, dynamic, and capable of examining ecosystems on local and global levels. But urbanization and modernity have incurred enormous costs on biodiversity, which is threatened in far too many ecosystems. The urgency to salvage resources has put fire in the hearts of ethnobiologists. We are rising to the challenge of understanding how native flora sustains human populations, and how human behaviors in turn affect ecological health. The pathway to discovery originates right here, right now, in this very time and place, in the fields, forests, and outdoor habitats that have sustained our species since the beginning.

In Missouri's Little Dixie, the study site of this book, wild flora with cultural value can be discovered nearly everywhere. The trick is in knowing where to look. Fruit-bearing trees are inconspicuous near tree-lined meadows, or nestled near the creek beds of shady forests. Hundreds of medicinal and aromatic herbs grow faithfully in unexpected places, like the cracks of sidewalks or the thickets behind the house. Depending on whom you ask, wild plants mean different things in Little Dixie. Some see pokeweed and dandelion as unwelcome intruders, some see summertime delicacies. Some see blackberries as invasive shrubs, while others see "black gold" in their fruits and strong medicine in their roots. Some see morel mushrooms as the tastiest secret in the woods—but most don't see them at all. Humans and plants are constantly interacting and responding to the other. Consequently, ethnobotanists have ample opportunity to explore dynamic relationships in their own backyards. Most plants we see are classified as weeds by horticulturists, but ironically, weeds comprise a very substantial category of pharmacologically valuable flora (Stepp 2004). In Little Dixie, these everyday species are not only valuable in the utilitarian sense, but vital to cultural conservation, identity, and expression.

Ethnobotany has borrowed methods and approaches from numerous academic fields: botany, anthropology, linguistics, folklore, ecology, economics, and cognitive psychology have all contributed significantly to its development (e.g., Cotton 1996, Martin 1995). The depth and complexity of people-plant relations has necessitated this all-embracing approach. The ultimate goal of ethnobotanical inquiry is to generate a story of continuity, of ongoing people-plant interactivity derived from "the natural, social, and cultural context in which the text is played out" (Alcorn 1995a:24). The new millennium will witness innovate efforts to examine relations between people and plants through multidisciplinary collaboration among scholars from many fields.

A great deal has been discovered about human recognition and categorization of the botanical world, especially through attention to "folk" systems of knowledge and classification (Berlin 1992; Brown 1977, 1979, Holman 2005, Hunn 1982). Relatively little, however, is known about what people actually *do* with their botanical know-how once they acquire it. Even less is known about variation in plant knowledge and classification within regional cultures, particularly in the rural United States. The pages that follow describe how people come to know about wild flora in Little Dixie, a place in the world where plants join other natural resources to sustain and syncopate human belief and behavior into a rhythm, one with ineffable meaning in everyday life.

Acknowledgements

This project came to life through the help of so many individuals, especially my graduate school mentors, Debby Pearsall and Mike Robbins, at the University of Missouri. Thank you, Debby, for introducing me to ethnobotany in the fall of 1994. Your invaluable guidance sustained me from the beginning and I am honored to be your student. Thank you, Mike, for sharing your illuminating mind and offering your companionship, and for fostering my appreciation for Missouri's landscapes and cultures. Thank you, Louanna Furbee, for piquing my interest in linguistic anthropology at precisely the right moment in graduate school. Gracious, intelligent advice was provided by Cecil Brown, Bill Balee, and Eugene Hunn—your work is my touchstone for ethnobiological research. My parents, Robert Nolan and Betty Linda Nolan, are my heroes, and I thank you for your faith, love and encouragement. Thank you, Robin Kennedy, for teaching me to recognize why plant taxonomy is critical to ethnobotany. Thank you, Mike Amspoker, for bringing biology to life so vividly in the field and the classroom during my undergraduate days at Westminster College. Many thanks to my trusted friend Mike Pennington, for the lessons you have taught me in the woods and beyond. Through a twist of good fortune, I found a friend in Katlin Jones, an extraordinary artist whose botanical sketches have graced these pages with vivid detail. Thank you, Marsha Quinlan, my sister in spirit, for reminding me time and again that laughing and learning are intertwined. Thank you, Alex Robling, for sustaining me with the friendship of a lifetime. I am deeply indebted to Mary Jo Schneider for her faith in my work at the University of Arkansas. My thanks go to Daniel Moerman and Brent Berlin, whom I have never met but whose work I admire. I extend my warmest regards to Gail Lawrence and Mary Porter, and the outstanding faculty and students at the University of Missouri's anthropology department. Thank you to the National Science Foundation for your generous support of this project, and finally, thank you to the good people of Little Dixie for entrusting me with your wisdom.

Chapter One

Scope of the Study

RESEARCH OBJECTIVES

This book examines people, plants, and their interrelationships in Little Dixie, a cultural region in Central Missouri. The goals of this study are (1) to document patterns of plant selection and use in the American Midwest, (2) to investigate ethnobotanical knowledge variation among the region's residents, (3) to determine the relations between folk plant knowledge and ecological availability, and (4) to examine folk classification of wild plants in the region. Collectively, these goals assess how ecological and social forces shape knowledge and classification of natural resources. What follows is an exploration of the role people play in the conservation of prairie biota, an endangered North American ecosystem. It is hoped that these pages will contribute to the ongoing efforts to reconnect social life with the natural resources that sustain it.

THEORETICAL BACKGROUND
AND RATIONALE FOR THE RESEARCH

The science of ethnobotany is rooted intellectually in cultural ecology, the study of human adaptations to natural environments, and in economic botany, the study of human use of ambient flora (Steward 1955, Plotkin 1995). Scholars have adopted these perspectives in tandem to advance our knowledge of human-ecological interactions. Influential works examine the evolution of human diet, medicine, and agriculture (e.g., Johns 1996, Piperno and Pearsall 1998, Flannery 1986), contemporary cultivation strategies (e.g., Conklin 1954, Rusten and Gold 1995), human sensory perception and recognition of

1

botanical resources (e.g., Casagrande 2000, Turner 1988, Alcorn 1981, Browner 1985), and patterns of variation in traditional ethnobotanical knowledge (e.g., Quinlan 2004, Quinlan et al. 2002, Berlin and Berlin 1996, Benz et al. 1994, Schultes 1986, Voeks 1996, Brown 1985).

Cognitive ethnobotany examines the psychological aspects of human-plant interactions. Cognitive ethnobotanists have investigated how people acquire botanical knowledge and how they envision and classify plants accordingly. Human knowledge of plants is dependent upon a number of ecological factors, including, but not limited to, sensory cues such as color, shape, size, and texture (Alcorn 1981, Johns 1996, Turner 1988, Browner 1985), ecological abundance (Kay 1982), secondary alkaloid content (Quinlan et al. 2002, Moerman 1991; 1994), and cultural constructions of efficacy and usefulness (Berlin and Berlin 1997, Etkin 1990, Trotter 1981, Trotter and Logan 1986).

Human beings are very adept at classifying the natural world in logical and practical ways (Berlin 1992). How people go about constructing categories, however, depends on who is doing the classifying. For plant taxonomists, classification tends to be a fairly stable, well-ordered hierarchical system based on morphological features. But for others, socially shared "folk" models take precedence over science. The classification of wine, rare coins, musical instruments, or automobiles is guided by the presence or absence of tangible and functional traits, such as strings in the case of musical instruments, or four-wheel drive capacity in the case of automobiles. Folk models enable anthropologists to interpret how humans think. They also reveal how information is acquired and maintained through beliefs (e.g., what is edible, what is inedible), encoded largely in the naming systems of languages. Hunn (1982) and Balée (1999) convey the pragmatism of native classification systems. Berlin (1972, 1992) and Brown (1977, 1979) emphasize the natural discontinuities recognized and named in those systems. Boster, Berlin, and O'Neill (1986) posit the importance of morphology in category building. Turner (1988) stresses perceptual attributes in addition to ecological salience, or the frequency with which a plant occurs in a given space. Sensory attributes also contribute to human recognition of plants with use potential (Casagrande 2000).

Applied ethnobotany has recently emerged as a subfield concerned with improving crop sustainability (Alcorn 1995a, Balick 1996, Estabrook 1994), organizing rural development programs (Martin 1995, Alcorn 1995b), and discovering pharmacological compounds in healing flora (e.g., Caniago and Siebert 1998, Elizabetsky and Shanley 1994, Etkin 1990, Schultes and Raffauf 1990). Moerman (1979) and Kindscher (1987, 1992), for instance, have documented the pharmacopoeia of Native North Americans, accenting the chemical ecology of plant food and medicines important to these societies. In response to the urgency to conserve both nature and knowledge, ethnobotanical conservation has mobilized national policies for preserving economically valuable flora and local knowledge of these resources, namely those which provide native people incentives for preservation (Balick 1996).

Others emphasize the cultural preservation of traditional plant use by connecting ethnobotanical knowledge to demographic variables (Nolan and Robbins 1999) and the continuity of regional folk traditions (Hatfield 1994). Insight also comes from folklorists and cultural geographers. In documenting plant uses among regional cultures, these studies describe various processes by which folk knowledge systems are transmitted socially and preserved culturally (e.g., McNeil 1992, Price 1960).

Relatively neglected, however, is the concept of intracultural variation in the ethnobotanical knowledge base of a cultural group. Recently, ethnobiological research has shown that the differences are linked to levels of expertise, whereby "experts" have access to more kinds of knowledge about a domain than non-experts or "novices". For instance, Boster and Johnson (1989) demonstrate that people who know little about marine fishes rely primarily on morphological cues when judging relationships between fishes. Experts make use of morphology and abstract information, gained through personal experience with commercial or recreational fishing. Although experts may prioritize different criteria when constructing taxonomies of plants (e.g., Medin et al. 1997), it remains yet unclear whether or not experts and lay people share a common ethnobotanical knowledge and classification system or maintain two separate, distinct systems[1]. Here, the structure of ethnobotanical knowledge among residents in Little Dixie is explored among residents with varying levels of interest and expertise in wild plants.

ETHNOBOTANY IN THE UNITED STATES

The vast majority of ethnobotanical studies have focused on traditional, non-industrialized societies, because the survival of these groups depends largely on ecological intimacy. Sadly, however, awareness of resources is eroding from collective thought and memory throughout the world. In the United States, the ethnobotanical record consists of a few excellent compilations of regional plant use traditions (e.g., Holmes 1990), but these works are scattered geographically and in need of theoretical synthesis (Jones 2000, Nolan and Robbins 2000). Wild plant knowledge is vital to industrialized regions, where biodiversity depends on safeguarding the wisdom of elders and the guardianship of family life (Wilkinson 1987, Nearing 1996). Ethnobotany now matters more than ever in endangered ecosystems, such as the forests and prairie habitats of the Midwestern United States (Samson and Knopf 1996, Nolan 2001, 2002).

Blending natural resources into daily life is a defining feature of regional American cultures (e.g., Brady 1990, Gibbens 1992, Williams 1995, Gillespie 1984, Price 1960, Koch 1980, McGregory 1997). Even in places where valuable knowledge exists, however, much remains undocumented. In his insightful compilation of Native American ethnobotany, Kindscher (1992:11) notes that the pioneer settlers of the Great Plains made little use of the flora in their immediate environs, adding that "plants from outside the region. . . and cultivated plants were more frequently used." Folk medical practitioners in the Arkansas Ozarks, for instance, maintain considerable knowledge of non-native species (Nolan 1996, Nolan and Robbins 1999). But these and other cultural groups are surprisingly unfamiliar with *native* flora. In Little Dixie and elsewhere across rural America, folk traditions like plant gathering are maintained for symbolic and economic purposes, while others are revised, reinvented, or replaced (Tuleja 1997, Janiskee 1991, 1980). In this project, wild plant use is understood as a socially binding tradition which links knowledge, emotions, and landscapes. The ways in which people are using plants in Little Dixie has been, and continues to be, the result of shifting social and ecological influences. Traditional plant use is therefore investigated as a regional tradition grounded in history and yet modified culturally over time.

THE CULTURAL CONSENSUS MODEL

To measure patterns of cognitive variation, the cultural consensus model is applied to the data. According to this model, when knowledge gained through experience is shared, a culturally-defined consensus emerges, which in turn differentiates "experts" from others. The model, despite its elegant simplicity, enables the researcher to estimate the cultural competence of each respondent, based on their knowledge vis-à-vis that of the aggregated group. The model is further relevant because it reveals the level of cohesiveness within social belief systems. In a compelling account of decision-making among expert healers and non-expert villagers in rural Mexico, Garro (1986) predicted and demonstrated that expert curers show greater agreement, or consensus, among their responses than the "novices," the non-curers in the village. In a very different study, Boster and Johnson (1989) showed how the model can be used to explain variation in knowledge of marine fishes. The novices from Boster and Johnson's study displayed more agreement than the experts, because they relied primarily on visual, rather than functional, information about the domain.

HYPOTHESES TESTED AND PLAN OF THE BOOK

Through a combination of ethnoscientific and folkloric approaches, the following chapters examine how social, cognitive, and environmental factors shape the acquisition and organization of knowledge among wild plant "experts" and "novices" in Little Dixie, a rural cultural region of Central Missouri. In Chapter 2, ecologic and socioeconomic features of Little Dixie are provided as a backdrop for the role of wild plants in present-day social life. The methods used for data collection are detailed in Chapter 3. The remaining chapters address five hypotheses regarding the acquisition, distribution, and expression of ethnobotanical knowledge. Chapter 4 details the wild plant domain with descriptions and sketches, and examines the geographic continuity of ethnobotanical knowledge. Chapter 4 addresses the first hypothesis: *plant use is not random, but guided by the human tendency to target species from "high-use" families more frequently than others.* Chapter 5 explores the second hypothesis: *experts should demonstrate more complex, abstract knowledge and appreciation of the functional uses for wild flora than novices,* and the third—*plants listed by experts should be associated cognitively on the basis of "function" while those listed by novices should be associated on the basis of "form."* Chapter 6 examines how plant knowledge is connected to the ecologic distribution of plants and tests the final hypothesis—*experts have more extensive knowledge of nonnative species than novices, who are most cognizant of only those plants in their immediate environs*[2]. Finally, Chapter 7 investigates the fifth and final hypothesis—*two ethnobotanical classification systems exist, in which novices classify plants according to morphological attributes, and experts classify plants by combining morphological and functional attributes in their cognition of wild flora.* The conclusion, Chapter 8, summarizes all results and their relevance for ethnobotany as a discipline.

NOTES

1. A number of works are readily available on expert-novice classification of cultural domains. Most research indicates that experts use complex, utilitarian cues while novices rely on mostly imagistic data. This has been found in the classification of ceramics (Kempton 1981), parts of an engine lathe (Chick and Roberts 1987), and physics problems (Chi, Feltovich, and Glaser 1981).

2. For the purposes of this study, the term "non-native" refers to those taxa which have not been formally documented within a given county of reference.

Chapter Two

The Study Region and its People

WHERE IN THE WORLD IS LITTLE DIXIE?

"Little Dixie" is the name given to the corridor of gently rolling farmland that straddles the Missouri River in the central section of the state of Missouri. In an historical account of slavery and cultural life in Little Dixie, H. Douglas Hurt (1992) proposes a map of the area that includes Callaway, Boone, Cooper, Howard, Saline, Lafayette, and Clay counties (Fig. 2.1). Folk regions are rather difficult to define geographically because cultural traits frequently blend together rather seamlessly in the US (Zelinsky 1992). The boundaries of Little Dixie are no exception. In his insightful work *Folk Architecture in Little Dixie* (1981), Marshall positions Little Dixie slightly more north and east to include Randolph, Pike, Audrain, Monroe, and Ralls Counties, but excludes the more westerly Clay and Lafayette Counties. To facilitate the analysis of county-level data, this study is based on Hurt's map of Little Dixie, which demarcates the boundaries of the region most clearly.

PHYSIOGRAPHIC FEATURES

Situated roughly between the Corn Belt to the north and the Ozark Mountains to the south, Little Dixie comprises an ecological transition zone encompassing 13% of Missouri's total land surface (Thom and Wilson 1982). Like the Ozark Region proper, Little Dixie is ecologically diverse, and supports between 80 and 90 native plant species that are absent or rarely found elsewhere in the state (Yatskievych 1999). The region consists of rolling hills, mixed-tallgrass prairies, and upland forests, where elevations approach 900 feet. Before the intensive timber extraction in the area in the

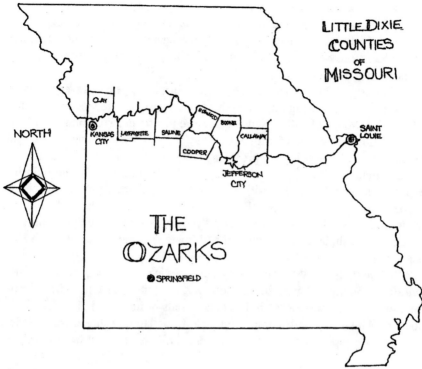

Figure 2.1. Map of the Study Region

early 1900's, the forests were largely dominated by native pine
(Yatskievych 1999). Today, oak, hickory, and cedar predominate in the tim-
bered hills and bluestem tallgrasses carpet the fields and savannas. Birch,
maple, poplar, and willow are common along the bottomlands of the Missouri River and its numerous tributaries.

SETTLEMENT HISTORY AND THE CULTURAL LANDSCAPE

As the name implies, Little Dixie is a region of Missouri where the stroke of
Southern culture resonates throughout the landscape. Marshall (1979:400)
describes Little Dixie as "a section of central Missouri where Southern ways
are much in evidence—an island in the Lower Midwest settled mostly by migrants from Virginia, Kentucky, Tennessee, and the Carolinas, who transplanted social institutions and cultural expressions". Many of the early migrants were prominent families whose plantations and fortunes were built
around farming tobacco, hemp, cotton, and indigo across the Southern US

farmlands. These aristocrats brought with them a plantation economy that included the use of slaves and commercial market crops. Other settlers of Little Dixie included subsistence farmers, merchants, builders, and teachers originating from Kentucky and Virginia. These people prospered throughout an expanding and fertile frontier.

In the early 1800's, during Little Dixie's formative years, slavery became an institution with lasting effects on the economy, social life, and architecture (Hurt 1992, Marshall 1981). Slaveholders frequently entered commercial enterprises through tobacco farming, but they soon expanded their agricultural base. With the Missouri River providing a ready route to large markets, a diverse agricultural economy soon emerged. By the mid-1800's, the industry experienced significant diversification. Cash crops, including corn, wheat, soybean, and barley, appeared. During this period, the commercial environment of Little Dixie gave smaller-scale "yeoman" farmers the opportunity to accumulate cash, land and slaves—the ultimate symbols of status in the Upper South (e.g., Mitchell 1998).

After 1860, the Civil War brought an end to slavery and the plantation agricultural economy of Little Dixie. However, the tenacious Upper South cultural heritage has persevered in lives and minds of its people. The following poem by Albert Edmund Trombly entitled "Little Dixie" (quoted from Christensen 1990) captures many of the images within this cultural landscape:

> It's the heart of Missouri, blooded of three,
> Virginia, Kentucky, and Tennessee.
> It's a tall spare man on a blue-grass hoss.
> It's a sugar-cured ham without raisin sauce.
> It's son or brother named Robert E. Lee.
> It's tiger stalking a jay-hawk bird.
> It's fiddler fiddlin' you out of your seat,
> Fiddler fiddlin' you off your feet.
> It's a bluebird singing in a hawthorn thicket.
> It's vote to a man the Democratic ticket.
> It's crisp brown cracklin's and hot corn pone.
> It's catfish fried clean off the bone.
> It's hominy grits and none of your scrapple.
> It's mellow pawpaws and the Jonathan apple
> It's sorghum sweetenin' and belly-warming corn.
> It's old Jeff Davis a-blowin' on his horn.
> Unreconstructed it rares and bites
> At touch of a rein that would curb its rights.
> It's come in, stranger, draw-up a chair:
> There ain't no hurry and we'll all get there.

Table2.1. Current Socioeconomic Profile for Little Dixie Counties*

| County | Population | | Agriculture | | Economic indices | |
	total	% growth	sales	# farms	ret.sales	% unemployed
Boone	129,098	+14.2%	28,780,000	1,344	742,606,000	3%
Callaway	36,932	+12.6%	31,435,000	1,323	138,223,000	5.9%
Clay	174,035	+13.4%	22,840,000	732	1,164,541,000	3.9%
Cooper	16,094	+8.5%	45,557,000	929	64,836,000	6.6%
Howard	9,733	+1.5%	26,186,000	738	22,804,000	5.6%
Lafayette	32,524	+4.6%	71,338,000	1,465	104,387,000	5.4%
Saline	22,890	-2.7%	68,482,000	1,083	106,246,000	5.3%

*figures based on U.S. Census Bureau statistics for 1998; growth figures estimated for 1990-1998.

Even to the casual passer-by, the distinctly Southern identity of Little Dixie is apparent today through the local dialect, antebellum architecture, foodways, traditional arts and music, and the strong influence of the Democratic party (Hurt 1992; Crisler 1948; Marshall 1979, 1981). These folk practices "reflect those brought to the area by English, Scotch, and Irish farmers traveling along the Louis and Clark Trail from the Upland South" (Skillman 1988). Agriculture remains a strong component of the present-day economy, although education, health care services, and manufacturing all contribute to its strength.

Little Dixie's more urban centers are thriving economically. However, the general portrait is a rural region with a deep sense of history and tradition. Rolling farmlands are dotted with traditional architecture, including I-houses with accompanying slave quarters. Dog-trot homes and transverse-crib barns tell stories of the plantation life of bygone days. The vernacular landscape reflects the present-day tenacity of Old Dixie folkways. Roadside restaurants boast of their prize-winning sugar-cured hams, served with black-eyed peas, black-skillet corn bread, and sweet mint tea. The rebel flag is proudly displayed on the walls of local taverns.

SOCIAL LIFE IN LITTLE DIXIE

Community life in Little Dixie is organized around a tightly-knit web of interlocking social relations that begin within the nuclear family. A strong sense of mutual trust and obligation colors ties between all kin, immediate and extended. Much like the rural Ozarkers described in James West's ethnography *Plainville USA* (1945), families in Little Dixie maintain certain clan-like features of social organization, whereby extended families—and in some cases, entire communities—are linked in spirit and history by common descent from venerated pioneer settlers. Several towns and villages in Little Dixie hold annual celebrations to commemorate their historic foundations.

While the family provides the basis for socialization, daily life reaches outward into networks of friends, neighbors, co-workers, supper clubs, churches, little leagues, and service organizations. These systems organize social relationships and offer support to individuals when aid is needed. When a child falls ill, for example, a mother may turn to one of these networks for financial support and medical advice. Churches frequently hold fund raisers in the form of bake sales or pie suppers to deflect the expenses for families in need. Children and the elderly are considered the responsibility of the entire community, whose members play an active and collective role in care-giving (for similar observations in rural Illinois, see Salamon 1992).

Conversations and informal interviews with local respondents revealed that distinctions in wealth and class are of relatively little consequence in Little Dixie. This is an interesting contrast to the farming community studied by West (1945) in southern Missouri, where rigid distinctions in social class were apparent (e.g., the divide between "prairie people" and "hillbillies"). Wealthy families in Little Dixie live quite modestly, blending unpretentiously into their neighborhoods. Social rank is derived not by wealth, per se, but through *decency* gained through honesty, hard work, service, and visibility in one's community. Decent people participate in voluntary groups such as the PTA, the Civitans, the 4-H club, church activities, Little League, highway cleanup committees, and other such organizations. Those who live "in the country" are conscientious about their weekly appearances at farmers markets, barber shops, diners and taverns, where social ties are reaffirmed and friendships are maintained through casual conversations. When individuals isolate themselves, whether by choice or by circumstance, rumors begin to circulate, for social withdrawal is considered a passive violation of decency. Hermits are avoided and regarded with contempt.

Daily activities in the towns of rural Little Dixie take place within a context of relative intimacy, reflecting what Freudenberg (1986) calls "density of acquaintanceship." Most residents of Little Dixie's rural communities are eager to offer help to neighbors and friends, and are quietly mindful of each other's daily activities. Care is taken, however, to avoid becoming meddlesome, for "nosy" individuals are distrusted. Local folks also prefer to associate with familiars when doing business. Independence and rapport are highly valued, and when contracts are formed, a handshake is preferred to a signature. Like other ethnographic studies of rural America that emphasize the unspoken cohesion within regional cultures, a powerful sense of place and belonging are evident (e.g., Janiskee 1980, Gutierrez 1984, Gillespie 1984). Community loyalty is articulated through social affairs such as festivals, parades, barbeques, pot lucks, raffles, craft ~~is~~ square dances.

WILD PLANTS, SOCIAL RELATIONS, AND GROUP IDENTITY

Although community-minded, the people of rural Little Dixie are devoted to a lifestyle of relative independence. Despite their proximity to metropolitan centers, they distance themselves from cosmopolitan goods and services. Children are taught the skills they need to hunt, fish, garden, gather, and participate in pastimes that foster independence at an early age. One way people maintain and express self-sufficiency is through the frequent procurement of wild plants for a variety of purposes. The majority of the plants gathered in Little Dixie are used for food or medicine, although wild plants are employed for a number of other practical uses. People in rural places appropriate natural resources in ways that articulate regional character and delimit cultural borders. Useful plants that grow wild locally are valued for their purity and wholesomeness, and, in some cases, for their rarity. Whether eaten as food, used as medicine, or valued aesthetically, wild plant procurement is a pattern that distinguishes locals from outsiders in Little Dixie. Talking about plants in Little Dixie is similar to exchanging stories about the weather in the "Breadbasket" of the Great Plains (Danielson 1990). Ethnobotanical knowledge provides a medium for day to day conversation and a platform for the enactment of rituals.

Depending on the season, persimmons, blackberries or wild apples are gathered from the woods and used to bake pies or to cook jams and jellies. Early in their childhood, boys and girls learn how to look for the best plums, strawberries, and elusive pawpaws in the woods. With these freshly gathered fruits, mothers prepare homemade dishes and desserts that fill the tables during family gatherings and serve as gifts for friends during the holidays. Pies, cakes, and breads are offered to neighbors in exchange for a favor or brought to local bake sales, county fair contests, or cake walks at school parties.

The use of wild plants and trees plays important roles in the social lives of both women and men in Little Dixie. To illustrate, a popular activity among men during autumn is gathering firewood from the forests for the family hearth. Providing physical challenge and a chance to socialize, firewood is usually gathered by fathers and sons on Saturdays. Teenage boys learn to identify hickory and ash, which provide the best coals, and the appropriate skills for cutting the trees and splitting the wood. When spring rains give way to sunny afternoons, local women scatter across fields and roadsides to gather burdock, lambs quarters, pokeweed, and other wild edibles. These prized greens are washed and mixed into salads or boiled into a leafy stew that is served with the evening meal. Others use the greens to prepare *spring tonics*, invigorating decoctions made from the leaves, stems, and flowers of medicinal plants by steeping them in hot water.

Using wild flora requires considerable knowledge of the surrounding landscape, the changes in moisture and temperature, and the growth patterns of vegetation. The knowledge required to locate wild greens, fruits, and trees outdoors is developed over time by participating in family walks outdoors, helping out in the kitchen, and listening to the stories of mothers, fathers, and grandparents. There is sublime significance in the sharing of wild plant foods in Little Dixie. It is at once personal and meaningful to receive a jar of mulberry jam or a gooseberry pie from a friend, or a savory bundle of pinecones and firewood from neighbors at Christmastime. Procuring wild plants demonstrates craftsmanship and reverence for tradition.

WILD PLANT EXPERTS IN LITTLE DIXIE

During a pilot study conducted in the summer of 1997, a number of wild plant experts were consulted. These experts reside around the city of Fayette, the seat of Howard County, and consist of herbalists (traditional and modern), medical practitioners, conservation activists, and local shopkeepers who market botanical products such as herbal medicines, oils, and extracts for flavoring food or making soap. The presence of so many wild plant enthusiasts in Little Dixie can be attributed to the recent commercialization of rural folkways and the conservation of cultural traits concordant with the farming economy (Mitchell 1998). The current interest in herbal medicine, natural foods and organic materials is evident across the backwoods of the American interior (Nolan and Schneider 2006, Tyler 1996).

SOCIODEMOGRAPHIC
CHARACTERISTICS OF RESPONDENTS

Table 2.2 summarizes the sociodemographic features of the botanical experts and novices consulted in the project, based on survey data collected during structured interviews. Data for the combined expert-novice group also appear in the left-hand column of Table 2.2. The demographics for each group are quite similar. Most participants are Euro-Americans between 30 and 50 years old, married, middle-class, long-time residents of the area. Several occupations are represented: farming, nursery work, and landscaping, which proba-

Table 2.2.   Sociodemogrphic Characteristics of Respondents

	both groups	*experts*	*novices*
	(n = 40)	*(n = 20)*	*(n = 20)*
Age			
mean	44.4	48.3	40.5
minimum	23	27	23
maximum	70	69	70
Sex			
male	40%	35%	45%
female	60%	65%	55%
Marital status			
Married	58%	55%	60%
Divorced	15%	20%	10%
Single	23%	15%	30%
Widow/Widower	5%	10%	0
Length of residence in home community			
mean number of years	36.9	35.8	38.1
Occupation			
Farming	25%	30%	20%
Storekeeper/Shopowner	23%	25%	20%
Teaching/Education	15%	10%	20%
Landscaping/Nursery business	8%	10%	5%
Conservationist/Naturalist	8%	10%	5%
Retired	5%	5%	5%
Health related professions	5%	0	10%
Clerical work	5%	5%	5%
Social work	3%	0	5%
Self-employed	3%	0	5%
Unemployed	3%	5%	0%
Ethnicity			
Scotch-Irish	48%	45%	50%
German	20%	20%	20%
English	8%	10%	5%
French	8%	10%	5%
Italian	5%	0%	10%
Native American	3%	5%	0%
Norweigan	3%	5%	0%
Welsh	3%	5%	0%
Unknown	5%	0%	10%
Religious Affiliation			
Catholic	33%	35%	30%
Presbyterian	23%	20%	25%
Methodist	13%	15%	10%

(*continued*)

Table 2.2.   (*continued*)

Baptist	10%	10%	10%
Lutheran	8%	10%	5%
Church of Christ	3%	0	5%
Christian Scientist	3%	5%	0
Nondenominational Christian	3%	5%	0
Jewish	3%	0	5%
None	5%	0	10%

bly accounts for the range of variation in botanical expertise observed. The ethnic and religious affiliations of the consultants reflect a blended cultural heritage of mostly Scotch-Irish and German ancestry.

CHAPTER SUMMARY

Situated astride the Missouri River in the central section of the state, the landscape of Little Dixie is ecologically and geographically diverse. Primarily rural in character, Little Dixie is shaped by a unique combination of pioneer ruggedness and an ambitious agricultural spirit. Tightly-knit communities are richly textured by independent lifestyles combined with a voluntary commitment to social support. Residents emphasize mutualism yet cherish their independence. A collective past has rendered a perdurable Southern identity colored by folkways which bind people intimately with their natural surroundings. Reliance on wild plants for food, medicine, and other expressive purposes is a salient aspect of social life in Little Dixie. Because of the role of native flora in the rhythm of life, and because the area has gone relatively unstudied, Little Dixie is an especially suitable location for this ethnobotanical project.

Chapter Three

Research Method and Design

In order to examine the patterns of variation in ethnobotanical knowledge and classification in Little Dixie, 20 experts and 20 non-expert (novice) consultants were interviewed. Most of the respondents reside in Howard, Boone, and Callaway Counties, which together comprise the cultural and geographic locus of the region. Howard County boasts a growing reputation as both a regional center for commercial plant growers and a hub for local herbalists. At least one expert and one novice respondent was consulted from each of Little Dixie's seven counties.

SAMPLING "EXPERTS" AND "NON-EXPERTS"

Biological knowledge has been shown to vary substantially among experienced or knowledgeable individuals (e.g., Gemeinhardt et al. 2001, Boster and Johnson 1989, Medin et al. 1997). To ensure an adequate representation of various types of experts, males and females of various ages were consulted, with both commercial and non-commercial interests in wild plant use. Some experts operate private herbal practices, others sell botanical products at stores or from home through mail-order business, or have contracts to cultivate selected species. Novices included male and female residents who have lived all their lives in Little Dixie. Like the experts, novices were keen to discuss their knowledge about plant life in their native region, and many of them roam the woods and fields to collect throughout the year. Novices represent the majority of Little Dixie's native sons and daughters, while experts are comparatively rare. Respondents were consulted after spending time in the region conversing with local residents about the topic. Experts were selected by the "snowball" technique (Bernard 1994) in which one informant recommends another, who in turn recommends another, and so forth.

Using the same interview protocol for experts and novices, both groups were consulted over two separate interview phases that spanned the summer of 1997 and the fall of 1999. The first phase consisted of a semi-structured interview with open-ended questions, free-listing, and a personal demographic survey. To begin the interview, respondents were queried casually about their personal experience with local flora. Questions included "how did you come to know about wild plants?" and "what do you find meaningful about using wild plants?" Most responses were transcribed by hand, although a tape recorder was used during many of the sessions. After a period of informal conversation, respondents were asked to complete a two-part survey. The first section of the survey included a free-list task (Weller and Romney 1988, Bernard 1994), an effective elicitation tool for ethnobotanists (Martin 1995, Cotton 1996, Quinlan 2004, 2005). Respondents were asked to write down the names of as many kinds of "useful plants that grow around here", and reminded to use their own judgement of what is considered *useful*. Respondents were then asked to indicate how each plant is used (e.g., medicinal, edible, ornamental), the specific application for the plant (e.g., heartburn remedy), the part of the plant that is used (e.g., stem, root), and the mode of preparation (e.g., boiling bulbs into medicinal tea). Appendix 1 provides a complete inventory of all listed species and uses elicited from the respondents. This process of successive free-listing (Ryan, Nolan, and Yoder 2000), provides a descriptive database for comparing respondent groups, and has been used fruitfully in a number of ethnobotanical surveys (Quinlan 2005). A survey was also administered to gather data on age, marital status, occupation, ethnic background, religious affiliation, length of residence in community, and length of experience with plants (e.g., Cotton 1996, Martin 1995, Hatfield 1994.) Voucher specimens were collected for as many plants named in the free-list task as possible. Each of the plants named in the free-list task were identified scientifically by cross-referencing common plant names and descriptions supplied by respondents with those found in local floral keys (Mohlenbrock 1986, Foster and Duke 1990, Peterson 1977, Yatskievych 1999).

CONSTRUCTING THE ETHNOBOTANY OF LITTLE DIXIE

To provide a comprehensive account of wild plant use in Little Dixie, ethnographic and ecological information on the 30 most frequently listed species was compiled from the interviews and supplemented by data from a variety of sources. Arranged alphabetically by family, each species is listed according to common and scientific names (see Appendix 1). With the aid of keys and field guides (e.g., Coffey 1993, Kindscher 1987, 1992; Kaye and Billington 1997), the habitat, flowering characteristics, and morphology were described. Because the name of a plant often reveals a great deal about its significance to people (Coffey 1993), the cultural relevance of the common names is discussed for selected species. Further, the social history of these species is examined by comparing their uses reported in Little Dixie to those listed in the pharmacopoeia of Southern Appalachia and beyond to the British Isles. A number of sources offer helpful information on important species used in Appalachian medicine and foodways (e.g., McCoy 1997, Williams 1995, Scott 1982, Price 1960), and others describe the role of wild botanicals in the folkways of contemporary Ireland and Great Britain (Logan 1981, Wilks 1972, Freethy 1985, Hatfield 1994). Material from these references is compared with plant use data obtained from the residents of Little Dixie. Taken together, these plant descriptions convey how ethnobotanical knowledge in Little Dixie relates to plant knowledge in cultural source areas, and further, how plant knowledge has been transmitted through time and space.

EXAMINING TAXONOMIC
RELATIONS AMONG USEFUL SPECIES

The free-lists were examined to determine whether plant selection is random in Little Dixie, or guided in other ways. To test this, the proportion of species belonging to "high use" families was calculated from each respondent's free-list (Moerman 1979, 1991). "High use" families are those that contain a relatively higher proportion of culturally useful species, while "low use" families contain significantly fewer. While it is apparent that some plant families are more likely to appear in the pharmacopoeia of any body of folk ethnobotanical knowledge, the extent to which one can predict ethnobotanical knowledge on the basis of plant chemical taxonomy has not been determined. Thus, a regression residual analysis was performed to reveal which plant families are represented. These results were compared to Moerman's findings to explore the roles of human sensory perception and culture-specific behaviors in plant selection and use.

INVESTIGATING EXPERT-NOVICE
DIFFERENCES IN ETHNOBOTANICAL KNOWLEDGE

The free-lists were measured according to frequency of mention (Weller and Romney 1988) and salience (Bernard 1994, Robbins and Nolan 1997).

Frequency of mention shows the level of agreement by dividing the number of times a plant was named by the number of respondents in the group. The software package ANTHROPAC 4.95 was used to perform the frequency calculations (Borgatti 1995). *Salience* can be described as the prominence or familiarity of certain items relative to others in a cultural domain. Though a number of salience indices are available (e.g., Smith 1993, Martin 1995), this study uses the measure B (Robbins and Nolan 1997), based on the proportional precedence of one designated type of item (e.g., native or non-native species) over another in a list. These measures reveal the content and structure of ethnobotanical knowledge held respectively by expert and novice respondents.

Experts' and novices' plant use patterns were compared by coding each reported use into one of seven categories: food, medicine, wood/lumber, ornamental, wildlife forage, handicrafts, and other. The proportion of plant reports that corresponds to each category was calculated for the experts and the novices. These distributions were compared using the index of qualitative variation (IQV), which measures the degree of evenness found among the proportions in a sample.

The level of positive matching among listed plants was determined for expert and novice participants using the corresponding program on ANTHROPAC. To generate the number of positive matches between the respondents' lists, an informant-by-plant matrix was created. This matrix lists the respondents as rows and the plants as columns to show which respondents (experts and novices) listed each plant. This profile matrix was converted to a square informant-by-informant similarity matrix, based on the overall similarities, or number of positive matches, found among the respondents' lists. Multidimensional scaling was applied to the similarity matrix to graphically depict the pattern of inter-informant agreement regarding free-listed items.

To explore the expressive differences in the evaluation of plants by experts and novices, a rating exercise was administered with the free-list task in which respondents of both groups were asked to assign a number between one and five to each named plant based on the evaluation of four different variables—overall appeal, usefulness, ecological value, and beauty—with one representing the highest and five representing the lowest judgment. The mean rating on the most frequently mentioned species was calculated separately for experts and novices for all four variables. Two kinds of analyses were applied to these mean plant ratings. First, the means for each variable were correlated for experts and novices. Secondly, a multiple correlation was applied to the experts' and novices' mean plant scores to reveal the interrelations between the variables and how they compare for the two groups.

EXPLORING THE ECOLOGICAL DISTRIBUTION
OF ETHNOBOTANICAL KNOWLEDGE

In this study, the plants on each respondent's free-list were cross-checked for availability in each respondent's home county, using Weber and Corcoran's *Atlas of Missouri Vascular Plants* (1993) as a reference. The proportion of available and non-available plants was calculated for each consultant's free-list; mean proportions were then computed for each participant group. In addition, the relative free-list salience of available versus non-available plants was calculated and averaged for experts and novices. These two measures were compared to illustrate how ecological salience influences the geographic span of knowledge and the overall degree of plant recognition exhibited by expert and novice consultants.

EXAMINING EXPERT-NOVICE DIFFERENCES
IN CLASSIFICATION STRATEGIES

Ten expert and ten novice respondents were revisited for a second interview, at which time a successive pile-sort task was administered (Boster 1994). Successive pile sorts are often used to examine cultural domains. They are especially useful for investigating classification patterns within expert groups (e.g,. Medin et al. 1997). Materials for the task included color photographs of the 30 species named most frequently in the free-list task. Some of the photos were captured by the author in the field, while others were reproduced professionally from the color plates of laboratory field guides (e.g., Kaye and Billington 1997, Foster and Duke 1990, Hunter 1984, 1989; Peterson 1977). Each photo was laminated with a plastic cover and labeled with the common folk name of the plant (e.g., wild cherry, morel). To perform the successive pile sort, subjects were handed the stack of photos and asked to arrange them piles of "things that go together". Respondents were instructed to create as many piles as he or she wished, based on any criteria deemed meaningful. After the first sort, respondents were instructed to examine their piles and to lump similar piles together to form (n − 1) piles, where n is the original number of piles created. This process was repeated until only one pile remained. Afterwards, the original piles were restored, and respondents were asked to begin splitting any pile that he or she thought could be further subdivided, to produce (n + 1) piles. The process was repeated until no piles could be further subdivided.

The pile sort data were examined using ANTHROPAC 4.95 (Borgatti 1995). For each respondent, a plant-by-plant matrix was constructed. The values in each cell of this matrix represented the number of times any two plants were placed into the same pile. From these matrices, two aggregate plant-by-plant matrices were generated, one for the experts and another for the novices. The cells of these plant-by-plant aggregate matrices displayed the *total* number of times respondents sorted two plants into the same category. Multidimensional scaling was applied to both matrices to produce a spatial representation of similarity for the plants named by each group. A composite informant-by-informant correlation matrix was also composed and plotted with multidimensional scaling to identify patterns of agreement and consensus between the two respondent groups.

To further compare expert and novice differences in classification responses, the cultural consensus model (Romney, Weller, and Batchelder 1986) was used. Cultural consensus analysis was applied to the pile-sort data using ANTHROPAC's calculation tools to explore the degree of variation for the combined group and for novices and experts separately. To determine whether or not the data fits the model, a minimum residual factor analysis was then applied to an informant-by-informant correlation matrix, which displays the degree to which each informant agreed with every other informant in the study. When the cultural consensus model fits the data, a single-factor solution emerges, whereby no negative values appear on the first factor and the largest eigenvalue is substantially higher than the second and the third (Romney 1999).

Each respondent was asked to describe how they decided to construct each category of plants in the sort task. These responses were categorized, and converted into percentages for the expert group and the novice group. A comparison of these percentages offered additional qualitative data for identifying and interpreting the overall classification criteria (e.g., shape, color, manner of use, etc.) used by experts and novices.

CHAPTER SUMMARY

Twenty experts and twenty non-expert residents of Little Dixie were consulted during semi-structured interviews, in which ethnobotanical and sociodemographic data were elicited. These data were analyzed in several ways to identify taxonomic patterns of plant use. The knowledge systems of experts and novices were examined using qualitative and quantitative techniques. Each free-list was also cross-checked for local species availability to assess the role of geographic distribution in structuring the knowledge bases of experts and novices. During the second interview phase, a successive pile sorting exercise was administered using color photos. Differences in expert-novice plant categorization were examined by applying cultural consensus analysis to the pile sort responses and by examining respondents' qualitative descriptions of their sorting strategies.

Chapter Four

The Ethnobotany of Little Dixie

A total of 187 wild plants representing 75 families was listed by the participants in this study. A composite index of all of these plant names is given in Appendix 1, which lists common and scientific names of each species, the associated taxonomic family, corresponding uses, and which parts of the plants are used. With a few exceptions, the vast majority of the wild plants listed occurs commonly in Little Dixie's seven counties.

Among the most frequently mentioned species across both groups include the fruits and berries of the Rosaceae, the rose family (e.g., blackberry, raspberry, wild apple), nut-bearing trees of the Juglandaceae, the walnut family (e.g., walnut, hickory), and various members of Asteraceae, the composite family (e.g., dandelion, sunflower). The section below discusses the morphology, habitat, seasonal growth patterns, and general uses for the wild plants used most often by the people of Little Dixie. Botanical sketches accompany a number of the plant descriptions. To supplement the following descriptions, references were consulted, including regional floral keys (e.g., Mohlenbrock 1986, Foster and Duke 1990, Hunter 1984, 1986; Smith 1977, Peterson 1977), folkloric accounts of wild plant use (e.g., Coffey 1993), and regional ethnobotanical studies of the Midwestern US (e.g., Kindscher 1986, 1992, Kaye and Billington 1997), Southern Appalachia (Krochmal and Krochmal 1984, McCoy 1997), and the British Isles (Freethy 1985, Hatfield 1994, Logan 1981). Ethnographic descriptions complete the overview of Little Dixie's culturally significant species.

CULTURALLY SIGNIFICANT FLORA

Blackberry (*Rubus* L. spp., Rosaceae)—Growing close to the ground as thorny bushes and vines, blackberry is one of the most widely used wild

BLACKBERRY
Rubus L. spp.
ROSACEAE

Figure 4.1.   Blackberry

plants in Little Dixie (Figure 4.1). A total of 16 species of this native genus
are found in Missouri. Blackberry patches can be found along hillsides, near
fenceposts, and on the edges of fields. In early summer, white blossoms give
way to small green berries that ripen to a deep purple or black by summer and
early fall. Blackberries themselves are coveted for their juicy texture and
taste, and when not eaten "off the bush" they are often used to cook biscuits,
dumplings, and pies. The roots are used to brew medicinal teas for treating
colds, stomach pains and especially diarrhea. Known throughout the Ozarks
and Appalachia as "black gold," blackberries have historical significance as a
favorite wild plant food of Euro-American settlers. In the British Isles, the
plant has been used extensively as food, medicine, and for its reputed powers
to protect the soul from evil spirits.

Burdock (*Arctium minus* L., Asteraceae)—Burdock is a favorite spring
green in Little Dixie. This European native produces fuzzy leaves, long
stalks, and clusters of coarse purplish burs. Burdock can be found in pastures, along fencerows, roadsides and in waste places. The roots are often

added to spring tonics, but burdock is most often sought for its young leaves, which are tender and flavorful when picked in early spring. Its roots have been used in Great Britain and Appalachia as a remedy for coughs and asthma, although the plant appears to be more cultural significant in Little Dixie for its edibility.

Cattail (*Typha latifolia* L., Typhaceae)—Growing in dense stands in marshes and along pond and lake edges, cattail is valued for its edibility as a wild vegetable. Growing four to eight feet high, the plant is easily recognized by its long, blade-like leaves, erect stalk, and brown tube-shaped flowering head. In spring, the cores of the stalks are eaten raw or boiled and steamed with butter. In the fall, edible flour can be obtained through an elaborate process of separating the starch from the fibers in the roots of the plant. Outside of Little Dixie, the cattail is known for its extensive use value, ranging from chair bottoms in Northern Appalachia to material used in the manufacture of alcohol in Northern Europe.

Dandelion (*Taraxacum officinale* Weber., Asteraceae)—Dandelion is a pervasive herb that can be found nearly anywhere, from lawns and roadsides to meadows and forests (Figure 4.2). Ranging from one to several inches in height, dandelions have sawtoothed leaves, and composite heads of yellow flowers. Both the leaves and the flowers are boiled and eaten, preferably during the early spring, when the flavor is best. Dandelions are also used in Little Dixie for making a semi-sweet aromatic wine. While branded as a "weed" by most Americans, residents of Little Dixie are well-aware of dandelion's use as a basis for spring tonics to fight allergies and boost the immunities. Called *pishamoolag* in Ireland and *Irish-daisy* in England, dandelion leaves and flowers have been widely consumed for centuries among country people of the British Isles.

Goldenseal (*Hydrastis canadensis* L., Ranunculaceae)—Goldenseal is an herbaceous perennial, growing 8 to 12 inches in height, with two palmate lobed leaves on a forked stem and a greenish-white flower followed by one or more small red berries. Found sporadically in damp, deciduous woods in mid-spring, goldenseal roots are steeped in boiling water to produce a purifying tea used for treating stomach pains and inflammation of the mouth and throat. Many Little Dixie residents swear by the healing properties of goldenseal and its strength in purging the body of toxins and impurities. Goldenseal has a rich medical history among Native Americans and early Euro-American pioneers, who used the plant in treating disorders of the skin, eyes, and ears. Over-collection has caused the plant to become relatively rare in

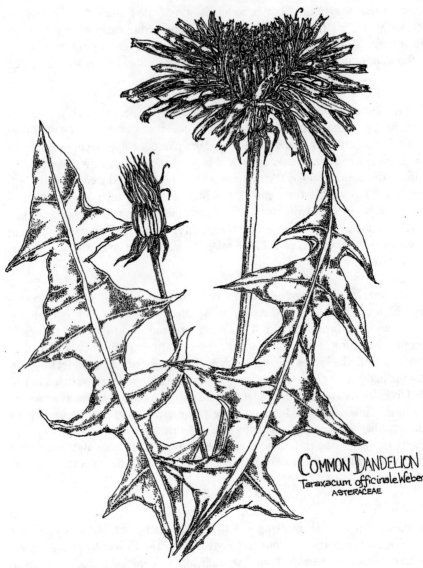

COMMON DANDELION
Taraxacum officinale Weber
ASTERACEAE

Figure 4.2.   Dandelion

North American forests. Goldenseal is now being cultivated commercially with some success in Little Dixie for its value as a therapeutic herbal.

Gooseberry (*Ribes missouriense* Nutt., Grossulariaceae)—Gooseberry grows as a low, thorny shrub on hillsides, in thickets, along fencerows and in other

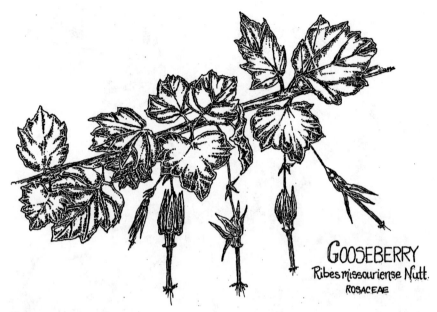

GOOSEBERRY
Ribes missouriense Nutt.
ROSACEAE

Figure 4.3.   Gooseberry

disturbed habitats (Figure 4.3). Gooseberry leaves are palmate and toothed, occurring in distinct clusters along the shrub's branches. Small pale-white flowers are replaced by a reddish-purple fruit that is sweet and slightly tart in flavor. In Little Dixie, gooseberries are known mostly for their food value. The fruit is usually cooked before eaten, providing a good pie filling or a base for jams and jellies. Gooseberry is an important plant in the foodways and folk medical systems of Appalachia and Ireland, where the berry juice is used to treat skin and eye infections.

Hickory (*Carya* Nutt. spp., Juglandaceae)—Valued for the quality of its wood and its nutritious, flavorful nuts, ten species of this North American native are found in Missouri (Figure 4.4). Hickory is used for a number of purposes in Little Dixie. Similar to walnut in appearance, hickory trees have dark, furrowed bark and compound leaves. Hickory is common in deciduous upland forests but is occasionally found in wetter bottomland soils. Native Americans produced a milky soup from hickory nuts, which the pioneer settlers quickly learned to enjoy. Little Dixie residents routinely gather the nuts, which are gathered and eaten from hand in the early fall. Some respondents enjoy hickory nuts boiled into a sweetened, crunchy tea—a tradition which likely stems from the Cherokee Indians in the region, who continue to process

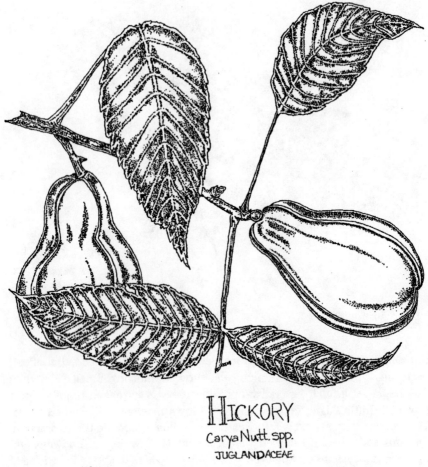

HICKORY
Carya Nutt. spp.
JUGLANDACEAE

Figure 4.4.   Hickory

and consume *Kanuchi* (hickory nut soup). The wood is also sought for its hot-burning coals, pleasant aroma, and the distinctive flavor it provides for smoking meats.

Jewelweed (*Impatiens pallida* L., Balsaminaceae)—Sometimes called spotted touch-me-not, this annual herb grows 2 to 4 feet tall, has elliptical leaves and spurred yellow flowers with red spots (Figure 4.5). Found in damp soils and shady woods during the spring and summer, jewelweed is widely used for treating poison-ivy rashes. Jewelweed is aptly named for its beautiful iridescent-colored leaves, which sparkle like an opal when damp in the sunlight. The leaves are crushed and applied directly to a rash

JEWELWEED
Impatiens pallida L.
BALSAMINACEAE

Figure 4.5. Jewelweed

to provide an effective and soothing poultice. Native Americans also applied the plant tissue directly to wounds, while in England, the local custom entailed applying its crushed leaves with hog lard as a soothing salve to burns and bruises.

Juniper (*Juniperus virginiana* L., Cupressaceae)—Also known locally as red cedar, this small, shrubby evergreen grows up to 20 feet at its tallest. Found primarily on rocky soils, along fencerows and in meadows, juniper trees have spiny needle-like leaves and produce a blue-black berry in summer and fall. Junipers are often harvested in December and used by local residents as Christmas trees, while the berries are brewed into a bitter tea used as a powerful laxative and diuretic. Juniper has a long history of economic use in Europe, particularly among the Highland Scots, who used the berries to manufacture gin.

Lambsquarters (*Chenopodium album* L., Chenopodiaceae)—Lambsquarters is a branching weed, growing tall and erect with greenish-white flowers and narrow, toothed leaves. This widespread, edible herb appears in disturbed areas, abandoned fields, and along roadsides during the early summer. In Little Dixie, the leaves of Lambsquarters are most often boiled and eaten with other wild greens—a food practice also common to Southern Appalachia. Native Americans of the Midwest also used the nutritious, albumin-rich seeds by grinding them into an edible flour. Lambsquarters is called *fat-hen* in England, which reflects the plant's local use as a high-calorie fattener of poultry.

Maple (*Acer saccharum* L., Aceraceae).—A large, impressive tree growing well over 100 feet, maples have palmate leaves, and somewhat glossy, gray-brown trunk. The fruits occur as paired schizocarps (sometimes called "keys") with winged seeds. Maples are usually found growing in fertile, upland soils or on isolated hilltops and meadows. Early settlers often used maple wood as material for small household supplies such as bowls, rolling pins and chopping blocks. Maple is still used for wood, and occasionally for the syrup and sugar obtained by inserting spiles into the tree as the sap rises in early spring. In Little Dixie, the sap and inner bark are used in cold and cough preparations, as a laxative, and as a constituent in spring tonics.

May apple (*Podophyllum peltatum* L., Berberidaceae)—May apple is most often found in damp, shady, wooded areas. The plant grows six to eight inches in height, and has a large compound leaf and a small greenish-yellow "apple." The fruits are edible when prepared into preserves, but the plant is best known in Little Dixie for it roots, which are used in spring tonics and medicinal teas for colds, coughs, and fevers. As suggested by its scientific name, may apple roots contain high levels of the drug podophyllin, used in contemporary biomedicine to treat venereal diseases. Native Americans and early Euroamerican settlers discovered how to use the roots of the plant to treat genital disorders.

Morel *(Morchella esculenta* L., Morchellaceae)—The lone mushroom in the entire inventory, the morel is the most highly prized edible plant food in Little Dixie. Morels are ineffably distinct by virtue of their unusual amber-yellow color and spongy, ridged caps. The habitat of this elusive fungus is the subject of much local lore. On cool mornings around Easter, morels can be found in damp woods, around stumps and dead logs, and in moist pastures. Frontier farmers in the Midwest soon learned from Native Americans that this unusual mushroom is an excellent food source. Morels are still considered a delicacy by locals, who enjoy them sliced and sauteed in butter or pan-fried in oil.

Mulberry (*Morus rubra* L., Moraceae)—Recognized by its reddish bark, mulberry can be found in various forest types, on pasture edges, along fencerows and in open lawns. The tree produces toothed, rough-textured leaves that vary in shape and number of lobes. Fruiting in late spring and early summer, mulberry offers a deliciously tart and tasty berry bundle, reddish-purple when ripe, that is commonly used in pies, jams, jellies, and beverages. Known mainly in Little Dixie for its edible fruit, mulberry remains a popular folk remedy in the rural British countryside, where the leaves are steeped into a medicinal tea used for treatment of intestinal upset.

Pawpaw (*Asimina triloba* (L.) Dunal., Annonacaeae)—Pawpaw grows as a large shrub or a small tree and generally occurs in well-drained soils (Figure 4.6).

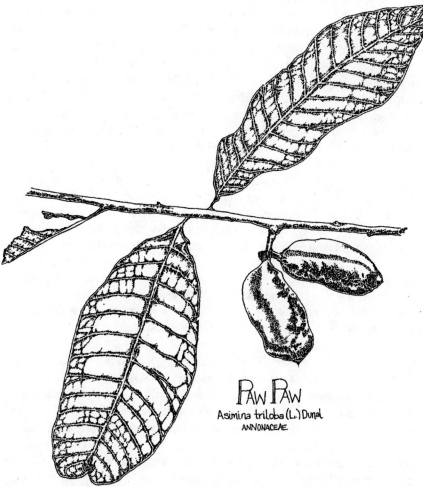

Paw Paw
Asimina triloba (L.) Dunal
ANNONACEAE

Figure 4.6. Paw Paw

Leaves are smooth and elliptical, and the 6-petaled flowers are brownish-purple in color. Pawpaw fruits are smooth, oblong, and somewhat banana-like in shape; the color changes from bright green to rich brown as it ripens. The fruits are gathered in fall for its delectably sweet and mellow pulp which is a favorite constituent of pies, puddings, and breads. Pawpaws are similarly delicious eaten raw. A North American native, pawpaws have a close cultural association with the American South, where the trees have special significance as a marker of regional identity.

Persimmon (*Diospyros virginiana* L., Ebenaceae)—Another favorite edible among Little Dixie residents, persimmon trees grow tall in old fields, in upland forests and other well-drained soils (Figure 4.7). The tree has dark, square-shaped bark and stiff leaves of an elliptic shape. Fruits are one to two inches in diameter, and range in color from deep orange to a scarlet purple when ripe. A favorite among deer and other foraging creatures, persimmon fruit is aromatic in flavor. When the fruits ripen in the fall, locals in Little Dixie use persimmons to make festive cakes and sweet breads—a favorite Thanksgiving dessert! Persimmons have a different history in Southern Appalachian folkways, where the fruit seems to have been used more extensively as a medicine for gastrointestinal disorders.

Pine (*Pinus echinata* L., Pinaceae)—Missouri's only native pine species, the shortleaf pine is a tall, evergreen, coniferous tree found throughout upland, well-drained soils. Pine cones are gathered and used as fire kindling, particularly the female cones, which are larger and woodier than the male cones. Strips of wood taken from old pine stumps also make excellent fuel for fire-starting. Young pine needles are reportedly brewed in hot water to make a nutrient-rich tea. The practice of using pine for food is known among Native Americans, but can also be traced to Medieval Scotland during times of famine, where country people learned to make use of this plentiful tree by processing the needles and inner bark into a crude bread.

Plantain (*Plantago major* L., Plantaginaceae)—Plantain is a European native found throughout disturbed soils, lawns and meadows in Little Dixie. This herbaceous perennial grows one to two feet high, has broad, elliptical leaves with undulate margins, and a tall greenish spike of white flowers. While the young leaves can be boiled and eaten in early spring, the leaves are used in Little Dixie primarily as an external bandage or poultice for burns, wounds, and rashes. Similar uses have documented throughout Southern Appalachia and the Ozarks. Plantain is often cited in British folklore as a popular remedy

Figure 4.7. Persimmon

for circulation problems and digestive disorders. In Scotland, the plant is called *healing-blade* for its widely reputed healing powers.

Pokeweed (*Phytolacca americana* L., Phytolaccaceae)—Also known as poke or pigeonberry, pokeweed is a tall, native, shrubby perennial with white flowers and reddish-purple berries. Pokeweed is extremely common throughout Little Dixie—it can be located in backyards, in neglected fields, or deep in the woods. The plant's berries and roots are poisonous to humans, but the young shoots and leaves are prized for their edibility. Many local people "safeguard" their poke patches, weeding them and caring for them year after year. The tender greens are gathered, stewed, and eaten or combined with other herbs to decoct spring tonics. According to Upper Appalachian folk tradition, pokeberries are combined with grain liquor and the concoction is taken to treat gout and rheumatism.

Purple coneflower (*Echinacea purpurea* (L.) Moench., Asteraceae)—Named for the conical shape of its flowering disc and its purple ray flowers, purple coneflower is not particularly common in Little Dixie but is occasionally found blooming in mid-summer along roadsides and throughout open meadows and thickets. Purple coneflower was used extensively as a medicinal plant by Native Americans. Prior to Euro-American habitation of the region, the leaves, flowers, and roots of this native wildflower were known among the Osage and Ponca Indians, who valued the perennial's anesthetic and immunity-building properties. Coneflower roots and leaves were ground and applied directly to a sore tooth, burn, or snakebite for immediate relief. Some residents of Little Dixie contract with wholesalers to cultivate coneflower for the commercial market. The flowers, leaves, and roots are prepared into teas and extracts used to treat infections and inflammation.

Raspberry (*Rubus strigosus* Michx., also *Rubus idaeus* L.; Rosaceae)—A medium-tall shrub found in sunny thickets and overgrown meadows, this European native has escaped cultivation in Mid-Missouri and elsewhere in the US With elliptical, dentate leaves and white flowers, raspberry produces a dark red, multi-seeded berry in the summertime with a juicy texture and sweeter flavor than its blackberry relative. Considered a good source of vitamin C, raspberry is widely known for its nutrient value. Raspberry leaves are boiled into a tea used to relieve menstrual cramps and pregnancy pains. The association between raspberry and pregnancy stems from Appalachia and Great Britain, where raspberry leaves have been used for centuries to give energy and strength to expectant women and to prevent miscarriage.

Sassafras (*Sassafras albidum* (Nutt.) Nees., Lauraceae)—Sassafras is a native, shrub-like tree that grows along fence rows, in open meadows and on forest edges (Figure 4.8). Leaf shape ranges from smooth (un-lobed) to three-lobed. Sassafras roots have been used medicinally by both Native Americans and Euro-Americans for many years. In Little Dixie, sassafras provides the basis for a blood-cleaning tea and a laxative. The aromatic roots of young sassafras trees are a favorite among many gatherers in Little Dixie. The root-beer flavor of Sassafras roots is distinctively pleasant and is used to enhance

Figure 4.8. Sassafras

desserts and beverages. Traditional root-diggers of the Ozarks and Appalachia have similarly procured Sassafras root for its economic value.

Sunflower (*Helianthus annus* L., Asteraceae)—Reaching up to ten feet in height, this North American native is easily noticed by its large, composite "head" surrounded by yellow ray flowers (Figure 4.9). Found in open pastures, meadows, and along disturbed places, the sunflower is used primarily for its food value, but is also prized as an ornamental. The sunflower is a symbol of Midwestern regional identity. A companion to other garden favorites, sunflower is also cultivated directly from seeds by local enthusiasts. Sunflower was widely cultivated as a food source by Native Americans, particularly those who did not grow maize. The fruits, harvested from the central disc of the sunflower in the summer and fall, are composed of tender kernels enclosed by a hard outer shell. The seeds can be eaten raw, but most Little Dixie residents prefer them roasted.

Figure 4.9.   Sunflower

Walnut (*Juglans nigra* L., Juglandaceae)—The most frequently reported tree species in Little Dixie, walnut is a medium-tall tree found scattered throughout hardwood forests with well-drained soils. Walnut trees have rough bark, ranging from gray to dark brown, and the leaves are large and compound. The fruits have thick green husks that enclose a dark brown nutshell. Walnut wood is valued for its durability and beauty, and is the first choice among woodworkers in the crafting of furniture, gunstocks, and household materials. In addition, the inner bark has been used by pioneers and contemporary folks to concoct a powerful laxative tea. While the wood also provides decent fuels, walnut trees are most prized in Little Dixie for their nuts, known for their excellent flavor and high protein value. Despite the enormous difficulty in breaking their outer husk, walnuts are eaten raw or roasted during autumn.

Wild Apple (*Prunus malus* L., Rosaceae)—Though dubbed as "wild" by the people of Little Dixie, the species referred to in this study is not really wild: its fruits are a domesticate that has escaped cultivation. Most often found in fallow fields and near abandoned homesteads, these small trees have grayish bark, elliptical leaves, and fragrant pinkish blossoms. Depending on the subspecies, the fruits range widely in size, color, and flavor, but are considered by local residents to be more tart and tasty than store-bought apples. In early fall, the fruits are widely gathered and cooked into pies, jellies, cakes, dessert breads, and cider. Apples were an important cultivar in Little Dixie during the early 1900's, though the fruit is no longer commercially important. However, apples continue to have symbolic value in Little Dixie. In Fayette, a picturesque town in Howard County, an apple festival is held each year to celebrate the historic and economic significance of apple growing in the region.

Wild Cherry (*Prunus serotina* Ehrh., Rosaceae)—A native tree of medium height, wild cherry is found in well drained areas, upland forests, and along hillsides. Cherry trees have rough, dark bark and the leaves are oval with serrated edges. Elongated clusters of white flowers are followed by dark, red-black fruit by late summer. Native Americans added wild cherries to meat dishes for flavor, or ate them raw as an energy source. The Cherokee and Osage used the inner bark to treat dysentary and labor pains. The pioneer settlers and their descendants in Little Dixie have similarly used the bark to produce a tea for cough suppression. Jellies, jams and preserves are made from the sour-sweet fruits, which also provide an important forage food for wildlife.

Wild Mint (*Mentha arvensis* L., Lamiaceae)—Wild mint is an aromatic perennial ranging from several inches to nearly two feet in height. The leaves of this Eurasian native are elliptical with dentate margins, and have clusters

of minute white flowers at axils. Most often found in wet, shaded woods, wild
mint is historically significant as a vital component of Native American and
early Euro-American medicine. While adding a pleasant flavor to teas and
cold beverages, wild mint leaves are useful toward treating a number of mal-
adies such as colds, coughs, fevers, diarrhea, and indigestion. Knowledge of
these uses probably stemmed from Native Americans and the early Scotch-
Irish and English settlers, who independently acquired the custom of using
mint-infused tonics as a cure-all and to relieve tiredness and malaise.

Wild Plum (*Prunus americana* Marsh., Rosaceae)—Somewhat smaller
than the wild cherry but similar in appearance and habitat, these native
plum trees grow in variety of soils, on meadow edges, and in dense thickets (Figure 4.10). Leaves are oval with serrated edges, and flowers are
whitish-yellow. The fruits, gathered in early fall, range in color from yel-
low-orange to crimson to dark purple. While some trees produce very
sweet fruits, others require cooking and make fine jellies and pies. The
bark of wild plum has been used in Irish and British folk medicine in much
the same way as wild cherry, namely in cold and cough preparations. This
use has apparently faded in Little Dixie, where the fruit is known solely for
its flavor and edibility.

WILD PLUM
Prunus americana L.
ROSACEAE

Figure 4.10. Wild Plum

Wild Strawberry *(Fragaria virginiana* Duchesne., Rosaceae*)*—Unlike the cultivated European varieties, the wild strawberry is a native to North America, and is occasionally encountered in the woodlands, meadows, and open prairies of Central Missouri (Figure 4.11). These low-growing, perennial herbs have dentate leaves in sets of three and small white flowers growing on

WILD STRAWBERRY
Fragaria virginiana L.
ROSACEAE

Figure 4.11.   Wild Strawberry

separate long stalks. Though the fruits of wild strawberry are smaller than their exotic cousins, they are sweeter in flavor and are excellent eaten from the hand. If enough can be gathered, wild strawberries make delicious jellies. Herbal practitioners of Little Dixie often use the leaves to concoct a vitamin-rich tea used as a diuretic and sedative. Native Americans of the Midwest similarly used the leaves to brew beverages and the fruits to make breads. In Britain, strawberry roots were used historically in treatments of venereal diseases. Frontier migrants learned to appreciate the edibility and medicinal value of the wild strawberry, which so closely resembles its cultivated relative.

Wild Onion *(Allium stellatum* Ker., Liliaceae*)*—Wild onion grows in moist areas, thickets, and wooded slopes. The native herb can be identified by its long, narrow leaves, small white flowers, and strong pungent odor. Enjoyed for their intense flavor, wild onions are gathered in early spring and their chopped bulbs are added to fresh salads and stewed greens. A number of folk customs of Appalachia and Ireland make mention of wild onion as a powerful (and magical) medicine. Native Americans also used the plant as a remedy for insomnia and lung infections. However, wild onion is used mainly as a food source in Little Dixie.

Willow *(Salix* L. spp., Salicaceae)—Reaching up to 90 feet in height, willow trees have soft, pliable branches and lanceolate leaves. Its genus name is derived from the Celtic term meaning "near water." There are 16 species of willow in Missouri, about half of them naturalized from Europe. Most often found along stream banks and in damp, shady woods, willow trees are used for the medicinal properties of its inner bark. The bark contains the compound salicin, the glycocide precursor to aspirin. Native Americans often boiled the inner bark of willow trees to produce a bitter, astringent tea to treat fevers and respiratory illnesses. Some traditional herbalists use the bark similarly to treat flus, headaches, arthritis, and other generalized aches and pains. The soft, malleable wood is also used to make beautiful chairs and benches, though this tradition has faded and is presently in practice among very few knowledgeable elders in the region.

ANALYSIS OF USE PATTERNS BY FAMILY

Having shown which plant species are used frequently by local respondents, it is now appropriate to identify which families of plants are culturally significant in Little Dixie. It is possible, of course, to calculate the number of reported species from each of the 75 families to determine which families are best represented. However, in Missouri, there is tremendous variation in the number of species representing each of these 75 families. Thus, a family with low species representation could "look" significant even if a couple of its species are reported. For this reason, regression analysis provides the best way to separate the most significant families from the less important ones. In this analysis, the number of species per family reported as useful is regressed on the total number of species per family ecologically present in Missouri as reported by Weber and Corcoran's *Atlas of Missouri Vascular Plants* (1993). The results are given in Figure 4.12, which plots the number of species per family in Missouri against the number of reported species per family.

As shown in Figure 4.12, the regression equation is:

$$y = .046x + .825$$
$$\text{with } r = .824$$

where y = the number of reported species per family and x is the number of species per family. The high correlation between the number of reported species and the total number of Missouri species from each family suggests that families with more species present in Missouri are generally more useful

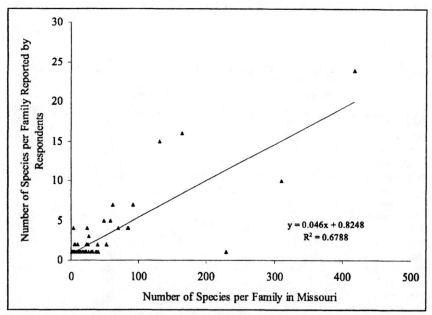

Figure 4.12. Regression Plot for Plants Reported

culturally than families with fewer species. However, this pattern does not necessarily indicate randomness. Moerman (1991) suggests examining the "outliers," or the families appearing above or below the regression line, which can be seen as exceptions to the regression pattern. In other words, families considerably above the regression line are exceptionally well-represented, whereas families noticeably below the regression line are significantly underrepresented.

A more formal technique for identifying "high use" and "low use" families entails an analysis of the residuals, obtained by subtracting the predicted value of the variable from the actual value of the dependent variable. To illustrate, there are 164 species of the family Rosaceae (apples, plums, blackberries, and others) present in Missouri. By multiplying 164 by .046 and adding .825, the outcome is 8.37 for the predicted number of species reported as useful for the Rosaceae. However, the data collected in this study shows that 16 species from that family were reported in the free-lists. Accordingly, the residual is obtained by subtracting 8.67 from 16, yielding 7.63. Thus, 7.63 more species were reported than predicted. In general, positive residual values indicate culturally important families whose species are more highly represented in the free-listings, while negative residual values indicate plant families with substantially fewer species represented.

The residual values for all 75 families included in the study are shown in Table 4.1, along with the number of species per family in Missouri, the number

Table 4.1. Missouri Plant Families Ranked by Residuals from Regression Analysis

Family	Number of Species in Missouri	Number of Species Reported in Study	Number of Species Predicted as Useful	Residual
Fabaceae	131	15	6.85	8.15
Rosaceae	164	16	8.37	7.63
Asteraceae	417	24	20.01	3.99
Apiaceae	62	7	3.68	3.32
Moraceae	4	4	1.01	2.99
Salicaceae	24	4	1.93	2.07
Lamiaceae	92	7	5.06	1.94
Polygonaceae	49	5	3.08	1.92
Liliaceae	58	5	3.49	1.51
Juglandaceae	26	3	2.02	0.98
Araliaceae	5	2	1.05	0.95
Berberidaceae	6	2	1.10	0.90
Oleaceae	9	2	1.24	0.76
Papaveraceae	10	2	1.28	0.72
Asclepiadaceae	22	2	1.84	0.16
Annonaceae	1	1	0.87	0.13

Table 4.1. *(continued)*

Family	Number of Species in Missouri	Number of Species Reported in Study	Number of Species Predicted as Useful	Residual
Morchellaceae	1	1	0.87	0.13
Phytolaccaceae	1	1	0.87	0.13
Plantanaceae	1	1	0.87	0.13
Cactaceae	2	1	0.92	0.08
Passifloraceae	2	1	0.92	0.08
Polypodiaceae	2	1	0.92	0.08
Taxodiaceae	2	1	0.92	0.08
Tiliaceae	2	1	0.92	0.08
Aquifoliaceae	3	1	0.96	0.04
Nymphaeaceae	3	1	0.96	0.04
Pinaceae	3	1	0.96	0.04
Caprifoliaceae	25	2	1.97	0.03
Araceae	4	1	1.01	-0.01
Corylaceae	4	1	1.01	-0.01
Cupressaceae	4	1	1.01	-0.01
Grossulariaceae	4	1	1.01	-0.01
Typhaceae	4	1	1.01	-0.01
Ranunculaceae	70	4	4.04	-0.04
Aristolochiaceae	5	1	1.05	-0.05
Balsaminaceae	5	1	1.05	-0.05
Bignoniaceae	5	1	1.05	-0.05
Ebenaceae	5	1	1.05	-0.05
Equisetaceae	5	1	1.05	-0.05
Pontederiaceae	5	1	1.05	-0.05
Betulaceae	6	1	1.10	-0.10
Ericaceae	6	1	1.10	-0.10
Hippocastanaceae	6	1	1.10	-0.10
Portulacaceae	6	1	1.10	-0.10
Anacardiaceae	8	1	1.19	-0.19
Cornaceae	8	1	1.19	-0.19
Lemnaceae	11	1	1.33	-0.33
Plantaginaceae	11	1	1.33	-0.33
Urticaceae	11	1	1.33	-0.33
Saxifragaceae	12	1	1.38	-0.38
Alismaceae	13	1	1.42	-0.42
Gentianaceae	14	1	1.47	-0.47
Aceraceae	16	1	1.56	-0.56
Ulmaceae	16	1	1.56	-0.56
Amaranthaceae	17	1	1.61	-0.61
Commelinaceae	17	1	1.61	-0.61
Caryophyllaceae	39	2	2.62	-0.62
Iridaceae	18	1	1.65	-0.65
Scrophulariaceae	84	4	4.69	-0.69
Brassicaceae	85	4	4.73	-0.73
Vitaceae	20	1	1.74	-0.74
Campanulaceae	21	1	1.79	-0.79

(continued)

Table 4.1. *(continued)*

Family	Number of Species in Missouri	Number of Species Reported in Study	Number of Species Predicted as Useful	Residual
Polemoniaceae	21	1	1.79	-0.79
Primulaceae	22	1	1.84	-0.84
Solanaceae	26	1	2.02	-1.02
Violaceae	29	1	2.16	-1.16
Fagaceae	52	2	3.22	-1.22
Rubiaceae	31	1	2.25	-1.25
Boraginaceae	32	1	2.30	-1.30
Onagraceae.	32	1	2.30	-1.30
Orchidaceae	37	1	2.53	-1.53
Euphorbiaceae	38	1	2.57	-1.57
Chenopodiaceae	40	1	2.66	-1.66
Poaceae	310	10	15.08	-5.08
Cyperaceae	229	1	11.36	-10.36

of species per family reported in the study, and the number of species predicted as useful according to the regression model. The plant families are listed in decreasing order of their residual values. Hence, the plants at the top of the list constitute the "high use" families and those toward the bottom comprise "low use" families. While a thorough overview of all of these families is beyond the present scope, the following section offers a brief discussion of the three highest-ranking families for use according to the residuals: the Fabaceae (the bean family), the Rosaceae (the rose family), and the Asteraceae (the sunflower family).

HIGH-USE FAMILIES:
THE BEANS, ROSES, AND SUNFLOWERS

According to the regression model, the Fabaceae, or the bean family, is the most highly represented taxon in the study. The Fabaceae is the third-largest family of flowering plants, and one of the most morphologically diverse (Walters and Kiel 1996). Most botanists would agree that the Fabaceae is a family of great cultural value, providing many high-nutrient food crops (e.g., soybeans, peanuts) and wildlife forage foods (e.g., alfalfa, clover). In fact, nearly all of the species from the Fabaceae reported by respondents in the study were designated useful as animal forage (e.g., red clover, white clover, lespedeza, etc). Very few other uses were given for members of the Fabaceae[2]. The Fabaceae are an interesting family from an economic perspective, because the taxon tends to be either highly used or essentially ignored cross-culturally (Moerman et al. 1999). In their analysis of five medicinal floras, Moerman and his colleagues found that Fabaceae is seldom used by native North Americans, but that the family ranks among the top ten most utilized families among various cultures of tropical Ecuador and temperate Korea, where the native species of the family are entirely different. The manner in which members of the Fabaceae are utilized ultimately depends on the ethnographic context—where, how, and by whom the plant is used.

The Rosaceae, or rose family, shows the second-highest residual value in Table 4.1. Like the Fabaceae, the rose family is highly diverse in form, occurring as herbs, shrubs, and trees. Though a moderately-sized taxon, constituent members of the family are highly significant from an economic and aesthetic viewpoint (Walters and Kiel 1996:222). Representing the Rosaceae are a variety of cultivated fruits and semi-wild food crops, such as blackberry, raspberry, and a host of other edibles including plum, wild cherry, and of course, the lovely wild roses.

One of the possible evolutionary strategies of certain species of the rose family has been to develop sweet-tasting, fleshy tissues around the ovary to encourage herbivory and subsequent seed dispersal. Other Rosaceae species produce secondary alkaloids, many of which are medicinal, toxic, or both. Moerman (1991:58) calls this the "poisoned apple syndrome," whereby some taxa simultaneously invest in seed scattering and seed protection by bearing fruit and poisons together. Ingested in small amounts, many of these poisons provide therapeutic benefits. In this study, a few members of the Rosaceae were listed as medicinally useful, such as wild cherry and blackberry. However, the rose family is represented mostly by species deemed useful as a food source, such as the plum, strawberry, and raspberry.

The Asteraceae, the sunflower family, is the second-largest flowering family in the world. Included here are a number of species easily identified by their distinctive flowering structure—a composite radiate head that resembles one large flower but is actually a composite of many tiny flowers. The "head" is encircled by colorful ray flowers, which serve as signals to pollinators. Some of the more familiar species include the weedy dandelion (*Taraxacum* spp.) and a number of cultivars such as sunflower (*Helianthus* spp.) and coneflower (*Echinacea* spp.).

In Little Dixie, members of the Asteraceae are used for a variety of everyday purposes, ranging from medicine (e.g., purple coneflower), food (e.g., sunflower, dandelion), flavoring (e.g., chickory), and transplanted ornamentals (e.g., daisy, bachelors buttons). In general, however, the Asteraceae are less known for their worldwide economic significance than the Fabaceae or the Rosaceae. However, a high proportion of Asteraceae species appears consistently in the *materia medica* of indigenous peoples (Moerman 1991, 1996; Moerman et al. 1999). The relative significance of this family, both in Little Dixie and elsewhere in the world, may be due to the morphology of its constituent genera. After all, when people single out plants for use, they respond to the same perceptual signals that attract insect pollinators and animal herbivores (e.g., color, texture, taste, and scent).

Other high-ranking families among the residuals include the Apiaceae (the dill family), Moraceae (the mulberry family), Salicaceae (the willow family), Lamiaceae (the mint family), Polygonaceae (the buckwheat family), and Liliaceae (the lily family). Several members of the Apiaceae are viable wild food sources (e.g., wild carrot, wild chervil), as are most of the reported members of the Polygonaceae (e.g., yellow dock) and Liliaceae (e.g., asparagus, wild onion). Several species of the Moraceae, such as mulberry, are historically significant as food sources, while the Osage orange trees remain important to farmers in Little Dixie as fast-growing hedgerows and wind-breaks on the open fields and prairies. The soft wood of the Salicaceae has little economic importance, but in Little Dixie, willow bark is still gathered and used for its medicinal qualities, while willow branches are used to craft traditional furniture. The mints of the Lamiaceae, such as hyssop and pennyroyal, frequently appear in the ethnomedical inventories of various cultures. In Little Dixie, these species are most often used for the treatment of respiratory ailments.

CHAPTER SUMMARY

This chapter describes the most culturally significant plant species listed by the residents of Little Dixie. Geographic continuity in plant use is evident when use patterns in Little Dixie are compared to the ethnobotany of Southern Appalachia and the British Isles. Because the relationships between people and plants continue to change through time, plant traditions are dynamic and in flux. Although a number of historic traditions have persisted across time and space, the settlers' interaction with new species has generated traditions unique to Little Dixie, like so many other regional forms of expressive adaptations encountered throughout the cultural landscape of the region. The regression residual analysis supports the hypothesis that plant use is not random, but guided by the human tendency to target groups of plants with greater inherent potential for cultural use. The Missouri plant families with the highest relative number of targeted species (e.g., the Fabaceae, Rosaceae, and Asteraceae) are cross-culturally significant.

NOTES

1. This use pattern indicates the perceived importance of wild plants in sustaining local wild game in Little Dixie, where so many hunters and conservation activists coexist—often in conflict!

2. The availability of any given species does not necessarily ensure its use. Take, for example, the Poaceae, or the grass family. The family is widely represented by 310 species in Missouri, yet only 10 of these were reported, yielding the second-lowest residual among all 75 families in the analysis.

Chapter Five

Ethnobotanical Knowledge Variation in Little Dixie

Understanding how wild plant knowledge is acquired and transmitted in Little Dixie calls for a re-examination of the human condition through a wide-angle lens. Our perceptual faculties and emotions promote awareness of plant domains. Accordingly, our capacity to process information on a cognitive level is what progressively guides our interactions with the natural world. The factors involved in ethnobotanical knowledge acquisition are addressed in the present chapter, beginning with an analysis of the plants and their corresponding uses in Little Dixie.

RESULTS OF THE FREE-LISTING TASK

In total, 187 culturally useful plants were documented through the interviews with the residents of Little Dixie. Experts listed a total of 160 plants, or 85.6% of the composite list. List lengths ranged from 12 to 61 plant names for the experts, with a median of 25.5. The mean list length was 26.4 plant names, with a standard deviation of 13.3 and a coefficient of relative variation (CRV) of .504 (see Table 5.1 for a quantitative summary of free-list results). For experts, the number of applications totaled 749, ranging from 14 to 88, with a median of 36. On average, experts listed 37.4 applications with a standard deviation of 18.9 and a CRV of .505.

Novices listed a total of 79 wild plant names, constituting 42.2% of the composite inventory. Plant list length ranged from 5 to 17, with a median of 10.5. The mean list length was 11.4 with a standard deviation of 3.8 and a CRV of .333. Novices listed a total of 221 applications for wild plants, or 22.8% of the total inventory. These applications ranged in number from 5

Table 5.1.   Expert-Novice Differences in Number of Plants and Applications Reported

	Number of Plants Mentioned		Number of Applications Listed	
	experts	*novices*	*experts*	*novices*
mean	26.4	11.4	37.4	11.1
median	25.5	10.5	36	10.5
s.d.	13.3	3.8	18.9	4.9
c.r.v.	0.504	0.333	0.505	0.441
maximum	61	17	88	21
minimum	12	5	14	5

to 21, with a median of 10.5. The mean number of listed applications for novices was 11.1, with a standard deviation of 4.9 and a CRV of .441. A comparison of the two groups reveals, as expected, a higher mean number of plants free-listed by the expert consultants. The difference in means, 26.4 plants listed by the experts and 11.4 for the novices, is statistically significant (t = 5.4, p < .001). Statistical significance was also found for the difference in the mean number of applications reported, 37.4 for experts and 11.1 for novices (t = 6.02, p < .001). Figure 5.1 graphically displays the

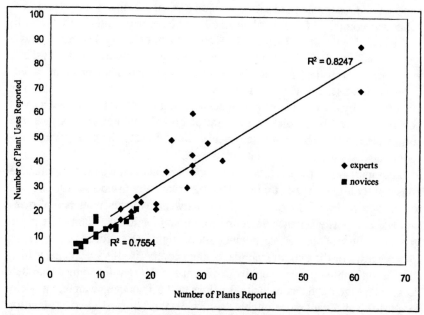

Figure 5.1.   Correlation of Number of Plants Reported to Number of Plant Uses Reported

positive correlation between the number of plants and the number of applications reported by both groups. As shown in Fig. 5.1, knowledge of plant
utilization rises incrementally with an increase in plant-naming knowledge
for both consultant groups. The number of plants named and the number of
applications reported are significantly correlated for novices (r = .87, p <
.001) and experts (r = .91, p < .001). While there is some overlap between
the levels of ethnobotanical knowledge demonstrated by the two groups, the
expert-novice distinction is reasonably clear, as indicated by the dispersal
of data points on Fig. 5.1.

THE SALIENCE OF LISTED PLANTS

The B values given in Table 5.2 measure free-list salience, or the proportional precedence of a listed plant over others. B is computed as follows:

$$B = \frac{n(n + 2\bar{n} + 1) - 2\Sigma r(n)}{2n\bar{n}}$$

where n is the number of designated subset items, $\bar{n}$ is the number of com-
plement designated subset items and $\Sigma r(n)$ is the sum of the free-list ordered
ranks of the designated subset items (Robbins and Nolan 1997). Here, a B
value was computed for each plant free-listed by experts and novices. To calculate individual salience values for a given plant on a free-list, $n = 1$ and $\bar{n}$
= (the total number of listed items) − 1. Ranging between 0 and 1, the B
value for a given item reflects the relative proportion of other items it pre-
cedes on the list. The B value for each species was summed across all lists
and divided by the number of respondents listing the plant to generate a composite B value. To calculate a measure of *overall* cultural significance, the
composite B value for each listed species was added to the proportion of respondents listing the plant and divided by 2.

A comparison of the experts and novices reveals that experts demonstrate
consistently higher free-list salience for the frequently listed species. The pattern shown on Fig. 5.2 plots the relation between average frequency of mention and composite salience value for commonly mentioned plants. Clearly, a
greater number of species has higher cultural significance for the experts than
for novices. For the experts, ten plants have composite B values greater than
0.3, but only three plants listed by novices scored a B value higher than 0.3.
As seen in Fig. 5.2, the composite B values trail off noticeably among novices
for those species ranked below blackberry, the third highest-ranking plant for
that group.

Table 5.2. Frequency of Mention of Plants Commonly Listed by Experts and Novices

rank	Plant name (vernacular)	number of experts listing	percent of experts listing	B value	cultural significance	Plant name (vernacular)	number of novices listing	percent of novices listing	B value	cultural significance
1	Blackberry	18	0.9	0.58	0.74	Raspberry	12	0.6	0.35	0.48
2	Dandelion	15	0.75	0.43	0.59	Dandelion	12	0.6	0.5	0.55
3	Walnut	14	0.7	0.35	0.52	Blackberry	11	0.55	0.4	0.48
4	Gooseberry	13	0.65	0.38	0.51	Walnut	11	0.55	0.24	0.4
5	Sassafras	13	0.65	0.38	0.51	Mulberry	10	0.5	0.24	0.37
6	Lambsquarters	12	0.6	0.34	0.47	Sunflower	10	0.5	0.25	0.38
7	Hickory	12	0.6	0.33	0.47	Pine	9	0.45	0.23	0.34
8	Pokeweed	11	0.55	0.27	0.41	Cattail	9	0.45	0.19	0.32
9	Plantain	11	0.55	0.32	0.43	Daisy	6	0.3	0.14	0.22
10	Persimmon	10	0.5	0.3	0.4	Wild onion	6	0.3	0.17	0.24
11	Wild mint	10	0.5	0.27	0.39	Maple	6	0.3	0.19	0.24
12	Dewberry	10	0.5	0.29	0.4	Morel	5	0.25	0.11	0.18
13	Sunflower	9	0.45	0.21	0.33	Wild apple	5	0.25	0.07	0.16
14	Oak	9	0.45	0.24	0.35	Oak	5	0.25	0.13	0.19
15	Burdock	9	0.45	0.27	0.36	Black eyed Susan	4	0.2	0.09	0.15
16	Raspberry	9	0.45	0.32	0.39	Wild strawberry	4	0.2	0.11	0.16
17	Morel	8	0.4	0.14	0.27	Paw paw	4	0.2	0.1	0.15
18	Wild onion	8	0.4	0.21	0.31	Marijuana	4	0.2	0.13	0.16
19	Mulberry	8	0.4	0.14	0.27	Sassafras	4	0.2	0.08	0.14
20	Wild grape	8	0.4	0.2	0.3	Goldenseal	3	0.15	0.07	0.11
21	Cedar	8	0.4	0.15	0.28	Hickory	3	0.15	0.07	0.11
22	Wild plum	8	0.4	0.23	0.32	Wild cherry	3	0.15	0.03	0.09
23	Wild strawberry	7	0.35	0.18	0.26	Wild rose	3	0.15	0.11	0.13
24	Paw paw	7	0.35	0.22	0.29	Honeysuckle	3	0.15	0.09	0.12

Differences in the plant naming patterns can also be seen in Table 5.2, which lists the 24 highest-ranking wild plants listed by the each group[1], the number of experts and novices reporting each species, the corresponding percentages of experts and novices who listed each plant, the composite B scores, and the cultural significance values for each species.

As seen in Table 5.2, there are more plants with higher frequencies of mention on the experts' inventories among the novices'. Consider, for example, the three plants mentioned most frequently by experts—blackberry, dandelion, and walnut, which were listed by 18, 15, and 14 experts, respectively. These frequencies are high compared to the three plants mentioned most commonly by novices—raspberry, dandelion, and blackberry, which were listed by only 12, 12, and 11 novices, respectively.

Three species, blackberry, dandelion, and walnut, were listed frequently by experts and novices alike, which makes sense because all are used in a multiple

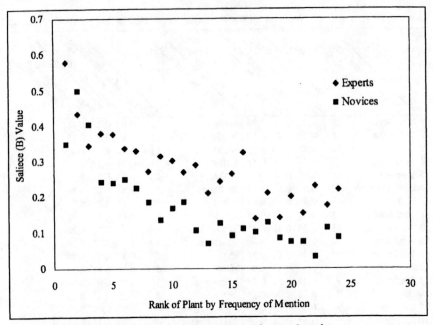

Figure 5.2.   Salience (B) Values for Plants Frequently Mentioned

practical ways (see Appendix 1 for examples). For instance, walnut is a valuable source of food, medicine, lumber, and dyes. Blackberry is also highly venerated for its edible berries, known locally as "black gold," for the food value of its young shoots, and for its medicinal roots that are often brewed into healing tonics to treat colds, fevers, and colic. The dandelion is similarly edible; its young leaves and flowers are eaten both by people and animals, and like the others, dandelion's medicinal reputation is well deserved as a remedy for chills and fevers.

Most interesting, however, are the differences between the experts' and novices' lists. As seen in Table 5.2, certain plants are more salient for each group. Pine, cattail, daisy, maple, wild apple, and honeysuckle are much more common on the list of the novice[2]. Similarly, several plants appear exclusively on the experts' inventory, including lambsquarters, gooseberry, dewberry, plantain, persimmon, and burdock. One explanation for this pattern is the tendency for novices to report plants with high perceptual and ecological salience (e.g., Turner 1988). Plants that are morphologically distinct, bearing obvious physical features (e.g., pine, daisy, cattail) catch the eye and in turn, are encoded more readily in the mind of the novice. Further, these species occur rather frequently in the ambient environment, and are encountered quite frequently in Little Dixie.

On the other hand, experts are more familiar with species lacking in distinguishable features, such as lambsquarters, plantain, burdock. Herbaceous flora are not immediately obvious to the untrained eye, nor are they particularly widespread in this region. Nonetheless, they are emphasized cognitively by experts, whose knowledge about their practical uses is apparent[3]. To illustrate, the leaves of lambsquarters and burdock are prized for their flavor, edibility, and nutrient value, and plantain leaves are used extensively by experts as a bandage or a poultice for exterior wounds.

THE DIVERSITY OF WILD PLANT KNOWLEDGE

Figure 5.3 displays the number of reports of use for all wild plant species named by experts and novices in the free-listing task. While the overall knowledge pattern for experts and novices is similar, this abundance diagram conveys a meaningful difference in knowledge patterns. Expert knowledge is more diffuse, as reflected by the higher number of unique, once-mentioned species listed. Consider the number of species reported by a single expert (93 species) versus those mentioned by a single novice (39

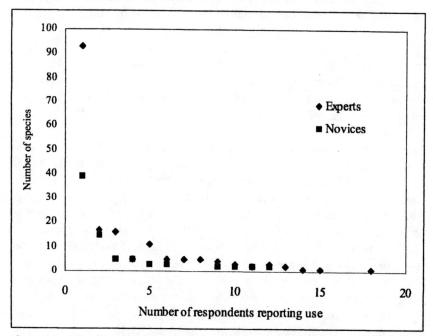

Figure 5.3.   Number of Reports of Use for All Species Listed by Experts and Novices

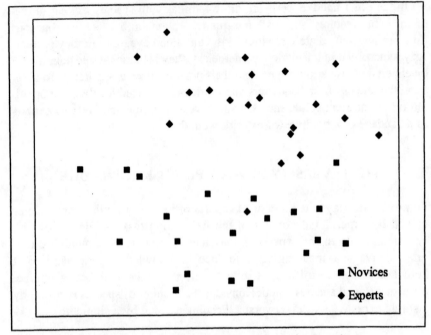

Figure 5.4.   Multidimensional Scaling of Positive Matches for Free Lists

species)[3]. The abundance diagram suggests that experts of Little Dixie command a greater scope of plant knowledge than novices, resulting in both a higher proportion of collective, commonly shared knowledge *and* a higher level of esoteric, idiosyncratic knowledge in the form of once-mentioned species.

From a qualitative perspective, the differences between the experts' and novices' free-lists are also worth mentioning. To graphically represent the similarity, the number of positive matches between listed items was calculated. The resulting coordinates were plotted using multidimensional scaling, a useful technique for visualizing relations between lists of items. Points represent lists, and those closest to each other in two-dimensional space are more similar than points that are distant. A clear demarcation is evident between the two groups. The plot suggests that experts share more listed items with each other than with novices, and conversely, that novices share similar listing patterns with each other. In other words, a common constellation of wild plants is mutually exclusive to each of the two groups. Two bases of ethnobotanical knowledge are therefore believed to exist in Little Dixie.

CONTRASTING PLANT USE PATTERNS

Despite a few similarities, experts and novice plant users in Little Dixie maintain rather separate ethnobotanical knowledge bases. However, the differences observed in plant use patterns are equally revealing. A review of the collected applications yielded a total of seven different use categories for the named plants: food, medicine, wood/lumber, ornamental, wildlife forage, handicrafts, and other. All wild plant applications on each free-list were coded with their corresponding use categories[4].

As displayed in Fig. 5.5a and Fig. 5.5b, food is the most common use category for experts and novices. In Little Dixie, edible plants constitute an important aspect of regional food traditions. The custom of gathering wild fruits, berries, and nuts from the local woods is shared and enjoyed by many residents, regardless of their level of expertise. The remaining use categories, however, are considerably different with respect to the proportion of applications cited by experts and novices. The second most commonly mentioned category for the experts is medicinal plants, comprising a sizeable percentage (38%) of the total reported plant uses by experts. The remaining uses given by experts were rather evenly distributed into decreasingly smaller categories of wood/lumber, ornamental, wildlife forage, other, and crafts.

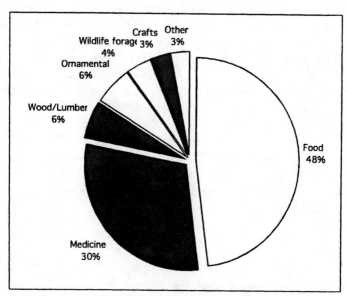

Figure 5.5a. Distribution of Plant Uses Reported by Experts

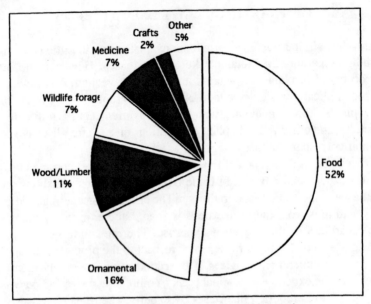

Figure 5.5b.   Distribution of Plant Uses Reported by Novices

Among the novices, the food category was followed by ornamental (16%) and wood/lumber (11%). The relatively high percentage of ornamentals listed by novices reflects their perceptual emphasis on wild plants. Ornamentals are deemed meaningful and useful by virtue of their physical characteristics and visual appeal. Knowledge of ornamentals is readily available through the appreciation of beauty and form. Comprising only 6.5% of the total uses reported, the medicinal use category ranked fifth in frequency for the novices, after wood/lumber (11%) and wildlife forage (7%).

To compare the overall diversity of the plant use categories for experts and novices, the index of qualitative variation (IQV) was applied to the plant application data. Ranging between 0 and 1, the IQV measures the degree of evenness in the proportional distribution of a sample. The higher the IQV value, the more uniform or balanced the distribution is deemed to be. The IQV is computed as

$$\frac{1 - \Sigma P_i^2}{1 - 1/k}$$

where P_i is the proportion of plant reports represented by each category and k is the number of use categories. For the experts, the IQV yields a value of .78, and for the novices the IQV is .79. These results indicate that for each group, the relative degree of evenness in the distribution of plant applications is extremely similar. That is, the seven use categories show a moderately balanced representation for each group.

While the IQV measures distribution or evenness, the index of dissimilarity (D_s) is useful for assessing quantitatively the differences in overall use patterns. D_s is calculated as

$$D_s = \frac{1}{2} \Sigma \left| P_e - P_n \right|$$

where P_e is the proportion of expert plant applications in each category and P_n is the proportion of novice applications in each category. The index of dissimilarity also generates a value between 0 and 1, where 1 indicates perfect dissimilarity and 0 indicates perfect similarity between the groups' categorical distribution. Calculating the index of dissimilarity generates a D_s value of 24%, which means that 24% of either group's distribution would have to change in order to match the other group's distribution.

What accounts for these differences? Recall that experts know considerably more about medicinal plants than novices. Experts are also more intimately involved and experienced with plants in general, and have acquired extensive understanding of the cultural uses of plants—particularly in terms of their therapeutic value. While it takes an expert to understand how to use plants medicinally, the appreciation of natural beauty is a binding feature of social expression in Little Dixie. Logically, novices are less aware of the esoteric, medicinal functions of wild flora, but are in turn quite cognizant of the affective, connotative, symbolic value of native plants.

PLANT EVALUATION AND APPRECIATION

There is reason to believe that experts and nonexperts share different expressive and aesthetic appreciations of the constituents of semantic domains (e.g., Chick and Roberts 1987), which may effect how domains are organized (Nolan and Robbins 1999)[5]. To explore these differences, a rating exercise was administered with the free-list task in which respondents of both groups were asked to assign a number between one and five to each named plant based on the evaluation of four different variables—overall appeal, usefulness, ecological value, and usefulness.

In descending order, the correlations between the rating scores for experts and novices are: ecological value = .70 ($p < .001$), usefulness = .49 ($p < .05$), preference = .46 ($p < .05$), and beauty = .36 ($p > .05$). These r values reflect the similarity with which experts and novices rated the plants, especially with regard to ecological value. It is noteworthy, however, that the groups do not correlate significantly when rating the plants according to beauty. These findings agree with those by Chick and Roberts (1987), who determined that machinists and non-machinists rated lathe parts very similarly with respect to complexity, but very differently with regard to beauty. Like the discovery by Chick and Roberts, these results show that the two groups agree most on the highly denotative variable, ecological value, and least on the most connotative variable, beauty.

Table 5.3 lists the intercorrelations among the four rating variables for experts and novices. For both groups, personal preference appears to be the most important underlying dimension in the evaluation of the wild plant domain. That is, plants that are preferred are also useful, ecologically valuable, and beautiful. One interesting expert-novice distinction is clear, however— the correlation values between usefulness and beauty. For the experts, there is a low correlation for the two variables (.39), yet for the novices, the correlation is very high (.92). The difference between these r-square values was tested and found to be significant ($z = 3.31, p < .001$). In fact, the difference in r-square values between usefulness and beauty is the only significant disparity between the two groups. This difference, taken in concert with the low rating correlation on the beauty variable, indicates that novices emphasize beauty in the conceptualization of wild plants. Novices are restricted to relying on perceptual stimuli when abstracting an emotional and/or cognitive impression of a given plant. It follows that a plant's usefulness is a function of its overall perceptual appeal. The emphasis on beauty in wild plant evaluation also explains the high proportion of ornamental plants free-listed by novices. On the other hand, beauty is significantly de-emphasized in the determination of usefulness in the mind of the expert. Experts command more ways of understanding plants in the cultural sense (e.g., nutritional value, medical efficacy, etc.).

Thus, it is evident that the accumulation of expertise entails a shift in domain appreciation, or how the domain is evaluated from an expressive point of view. The rating patterns by the two groups strongly imply that experts

Table 5.3.   Multiple Correlation of Mean Ranks of Wild Plants on Four Variables

Variable	*Preference*	*Usefulness*	*Ecological Value*	*Beauty*
Preference	1			
Usefulness	0.72*** (0.68)***	1		
Ecological value	0.74*** (0.78)***	0.55* (0.44)*	1	
Beauty	0.62** (0.66)**	0.39 (0.92)***	0.68** (0.57)**	1

***p < .001, **p < .01, *p < .05

and novices have contrasting aesthetic standards for wild plants, which appears to be linked to underlying differences in how the domain is conceptually organized.

CHAPTER SUMMARY

While there is some overlap in the ethnobotanical knowledge bases of the experts and novices, it has been shown, as predicted, that each group maintains a fairly distinct system of wild plant knowledge. Each system can be understood by examining the plants and uses cited in the free-lists, which reflect how experts and novices acquire and develop information about ambient flora. The data suggest that novices are more cognizant of plants with high perceptual and ecological salience, while experts display shared knowledge of species that are less obvious perceptually and abundant ecologically but with high use potential. The manner in which each group uses wild plants is equally diverse, with food representing the major use category. What sets the experts apart from the novices, however, are the qualitative use patterns observed. Experts use a higher proportion of plants for medicinal purposes. Novices emphasize beauty, while experts prioritize ecological value, a function-based variable, when ranking the plants. Thus, experts are influenced most by practicality, while the others with less experience are affected by imagistic variables such as color, size, and shape. Taken together, all of these results suggest that knowledge begins with perceptual factors and guided progressively by aesthetic factors, while expertise engenders a more complex comprehension of plants based on utilitarian factors acquired through time.

NOTES

1. Twenty four plants seemed logical because this number represents a natural break in the descending frequencies of plant names recorded.

2. These plants are not absent altogether from the experts' wild plant inventory; they appear further down on the composite list (see Appendix 1). The reduced salience of these plants among experts suggests that these species have less practical importance and cultural significance on the expert level.

3. Similar use report patterns by plant experts appear throughout the ethnobotanical literature. For example, in a study of Mestizo plant use in rural Mexico by Benz and his colleagues (1994), a high number of once-mentioned species was listed by expert consultants. Accordingly, Nolan (1996) found that wild plant experts of the Ozark-Ouachita Highlands listed relatively high proportions of "unique" species. Ethnobotanical research frequently finds considerable knowledge dispersal among expert

respondents. These studies offer a challenge to cultural consensus theory, which is built on the proposition that consensus reflects the culturally defined truth.

4. The boundaries between certain use categories are often "fuzzy," particularly with respect to food and medicine. For this reason, it was necessary to code a number of plants into multiple categories, such as those used in spring tonics (e.g., sassafras, burdock, may apple). For more information on the categorical overlap of food and medicine in people-plant interactions, see Johns (1994).

5. For example, Chick and Roberts (1987) examined the evaluation of lathe parts by machinists and nonmachinists. The authors discovered that the machinists display more agreement regarding the expressive aspects of lathe parts than the non-machinists, due to the experts' better understanding of how the parts are manufactured.

Chapter Six

The Ecology of
Ethnobotanical Knowledge

To what extent is knowledge actually crafted by our ecological surroundings? Up to now it has been shown that residents of Little Dixie share two separate ethnobotanical knowledge systems, based primarily on differing perceptions of usefulness. What remains to be shown, however, is the manner by which experts and novices contrast in their awareness of *ambient* plant species—the trees, shrubs, vines, and herbs actually seen in Little Dixie every day. Upon first inspection, it would appear that plants that are highly abundant, or ecologically salient, are most likely to be known. However, Kindscher (1987, 1992) has observed that the early Midwestern pioneers knew relatively little about native prairie plants. In a different study, plant experts of the Ozarks showed knowledge of numerous medicinal plants that are not native to their region of residence (Nolan 1996). This was attributed to the present-day movement of people and the subsequent flow of information between different ecological zones. One might wonder why plants with low accessibility have cultural significance in the first place. Turner (1988:90) explains that plants such as these capture peoples' attention when they "possess other important or distinctive features that offset their low availability". In terms of knowledge variation, these findings suggest that the experts' interest and experience with plants should lead them to know more than novices about nonnative types that grow far from their homes.

The geographic distribution of all 187 free-listed species in Little Dixie's seven counties was determined by consulting Weber and Corcoran's *Atlas of Missouri Vascular Plants* (1993), which documents which species have been collected in each county of the state. A plant-by-county spreadsheet was created that illustrates species collected in each county.

To test the hypothesis, two kinds of analyses were applied. For each of the experts' and novices' free-lists, the percent of native versus non-native species was determined as well as the relative free-list salience of native and non-native species. If the hypothesis holds, then the experts should list a significantly higher mean proportion of non-native species than novices, and should likewise show a higher overall salience value for non-native species than novices.

FREE-LIST PROPORTIONS OF NATIVE AND NON-NATIVE SPECIES

For each respondent's free-list, the number of species previously documented in his or her home county was summed and divided by the total number of species on the free-list. These proportions were summed separately for experts and novices and divided by 20 to obtain a mean proportion of native (and non-native) species listed by each group. The results of the calculations are summarized in Table 6.1.

On average, both groups listed a very high percentage of native species and a very small proportion of plants non-native to their respective counties of origin. As seen in Table 6.1, experts reported a mean of .867 native species and .133 non-native species per list, while novices averaged .956 native types and .044 exotic plants on their free-lists. Each of these proportions differs significantly from .5, which would result if native and non-native species were distributed equally in the free-lists. These differences are indicated by a z-test: for the experts, $z = 3.28$ ($p < .001$) and for novices, $z = 4.08$, ($p < .001$). While experts listed a slightly higher percentage of ecologically unavailable species than novices, this provides only moderate support for the proposition that expert respondents are more knowledgeable about those taxa than novices. A difference of proportions test (Zar 1974:296-198) was applied to these values, which yielded no significant difference between the two percentages ($z = -.99$, $p > .05$).

Table 6.1. Ecological Salience of Species Listed by Experts and Novices

	experts	novices
Mean proportion of native species listed	0.867**	0.956**
Mean proportion of non-native species listed	0.133	0.044
Mean salience of native species listed (B_{native})	0.723*	0.903**
Mean salience of non-native species listed ($B_{non-native}$)	0.277	0.097
	*p < .05, **p < .001	

FREE-LIST SALIENCE OF NATIVE AND NONNATIVE SPECIES

The categorical salience measure B was computed for native and nonnative species on each respondent's free-list. This provided a systematic method of examining expert-novice differences in the relative free-list salience of locally available versus exotic species. For both experts and novices, the summed B values were divided by 20 to generate a mean proportional salience index of native versus non-native species on the lists. These mean salience values, denoted by B_{native} and $B_{non-native}$, are given for experts and novices in Table 6.1.

For both groups, native species are shown to be much more salient than non-native plants. This is especially true for the novices, whose mean B_{native} value of .903 (and mean $B_{non-native}$ value of .097) reflect considerable cognitive privileging of the plant taxa that are present in their environment. Interestingly, experts also give mental priority to those taxa native to their home counties, as indicated by their mean B_{native} value of .723 (and mean $B_{non-native}$ value of .277). Using the z-test, each of these proportions are found to differ significantly from .5 (for experts, $z = 1.99$, $p < .05$; for novices, $z = 3.60$, $p < .001$). Once again, the difference of proportions test does not yield a significant difference between the salience of native versus non-native plants listed by experts and novices ($z = -1.46$, $p > .05$).

EXPERTISE AND ECOLOGICAL AVAILABILITY

The first pattern that emerges in this analysis pertains to the plants themselves. The vast majority of the plants used in Little Dixie are ecologically present in the counties in which they were reported. That is, there are relatively few instances in which respondents free-listed a plant that has not been documented geographically in his or her home county. The high mean percentages of native plants free-listed by experts and novices further supports this observation.

Of the ecologically unavailable plants that were reported, only 3 species, currant (*Ribes odoratum*), sarsaparilla (*Aralia nudicaulis*), and passion flower (*Passiflora incarnata*), were listed by more than one respondent. However, these plants were mentioned by multiple expert respondents and deserve further mention. Though common in the Ozark Region to the south, currant, sarsaparilla, and passion flower do not grow in any of the 7 Little Dixie counties. To understand why these exotic plants were reported by multiple experts, it helps to look on the shelves of the local botanical supply shops. Passion flower is promoted at local herbal shops as a natural sedative and homeopathic sleep-aid.

The aromatic sarsaparilla and currant are popular flavorings in beverages, liqueurs, and other products. In general, it is quite likely that the commercial availability and local cultural appeal of these botanicals accounts for their appearance on the free-lists.

Returning to the data, the calculations suggest that experts know about and use a slightly higher number of ecologically remote species than novices. With the exception of the species discussed above, however, plants that do not grow locally are not culturally pervasive in Little Dixie. Although non-native plants are moderately more salient for the experts than the novices, the analysis indicates that experts do not demonstrate any significant cognitive privileging of exotic plants in their free-lists. In rare instances when novices did list exotic species, these items show low salience, appearing toward the bottom of their plant lists.

While the frontier settlers of the Midwestern prairie region may not have fully exploited the plants that were available to them, the contemporary residents of Little Dixie are quite knowledgeable about the plants around them. These results contrast with previous research indicating that expert plant users have extensive knowledge of non-native species (Nolan 1996). One possible explanation for the disagreement lies in how the wild plant domain is delimited in these studies. When the inquiry is expanded to include *all* the potential uses for wild flora—as this study has done—it appears that native species are prioritized over introduced varieties in the total plant inventory. When the entire domain of useful wild plants is elicited, respondents tend to narrow their ecological focus, listing primarily those species apparent in their immediate locales. However, when the domain is restricted, for example, to one or two aspects of use (e.g., medicinal or edible plants), rare and ecologically remote species are elicited.

CHAPTER SUMMARY

Analysis of the spatial distribution of listed plants reveals only a tenuous link between knowledge variation and species availability. When experts' and novices' free-lists are compared, it is shown that experts are slightly, though not significantly, more knowledgeable about non-native species than novices. Further, it appears that both respondent groups—particularly the novices—are most cognizant of the species that occur locally than others. Contrary to the hypothesis that non-native plants are culturally salient to plant users in rural America, the overall pattern suggests that people are most familiar about the uses for species that are readily accessible in the habitats that surround them.

Chapter Seven

Ethnobotanical Categorization among Experts and Novices

"the only difference between a flower and a weed is discrimination"

—Anonymous

The "folk" classification of living things is a fascinating phenomenon. Understanding cognition is crucial toward understanding why humans faithfully designate related things to named categories. When categorical relationships emerge between "types of medicines" or "kinds of trees", important cultural beliefs begin to appear. Botanists are keen on locating genetic links between plants in a systematic fashion. Ethnobotanists are equally interested in understanding why people envision, name, and classify plants in rather similar ways—even without formal taxonomic training. Why do squashes, gourds, and pumpkins share a certain essence? Is it their texture and shape, or their tendency to sprawl in rambling patches? And why does the tomato exist in that fuzzy borderland between fruits and vegetables? Discovering linkages between biological and cultural reality is a salient goal for ethnobotany, calling for a closer look at how plants, as a cultural domain, are rendered meaningful. Wild plant classification in Little Dixie constitutes the focus of the present chapter.

THE SUCCESSIVE PILE SORT TASK

To examine the content of plant categories and their cognitive arrangement, ten experts and ten novices were consulted for a second interview and asked to complete a successive pile-sort task (Martin 1995, Boster 1994, Weller and Romney 1988). Respondents were handed a stack of 30 photographs of wild plants (Table 7.1) and asked to sort them into as many piles as they wished,

63

Table 7.1. Wild Plant Species Used in Pile Sort Task

Common name	Scientific name	Family name
Blackberry	*Rubus* spp.	Rosaceae
Dandelion	*Taraxacum officinale* Weber.	Asteraceae
Walnut	*Juglans* spp.	Juglandaceae
Raspberry	*Rubus strigosus* Michx.	Rosaceae
Sunflower	*Helianthus annuus* L.	Asteraceae
Mulberry	*Morus rubra* L.	Moraceae
Sassafras	*Sassafras albidum* (Nutt.) Nees.	Lauraceae
Hickory	*Carya* spp.	Juglandaceae
Gooseberry	*Ribes missouriense* Nutt.	Grossulariaceae
Oak	*Quercus* spp.	Fagaceae
Juniper	*Juniperus virginiana* L.	Cupressaceae
Lambsquarters	*Chenopodium album* L.	Chenopodiaceae
Cattail	*Typha latifolia*	Typhaceae
Wild onion	*Allium stellatum* Ker.	Liliaceae
Pine	*Pinus echinata* L.	Pinaceae
Morel	*Morchella esculenta* L.	Morchellaceae
Apple	*Prunus malus* L.	Rosaceae
Persimmon	*Diospyros virginiana* L.	Ebenaceae
Paw paw	*Asimina triloba* (L.) Dunal	Annonaceae
Pokeweed	*Phytolacca americana* L.	Phytolaccaceae
Wild mint	*Mentha arvensis* L.	Lamiaceae
Wild strawberry	*Fragaria* spp.	Rosaceae
Plantain	*Plantago major* L.	Plantaginaceae
Wild cherry	*Prunus* spp.	Rosaceae
Dewberry	*Rubus flagellaris* Willd.	Rosaceae
Maple	*Acer saccharum* L.	Aceraceae
Burdock	*Arctium minus* Bernh.	Asteraceae
Wild plum	*Prunus americana* Marsh.	Rosaceae
Purple coneflower	*Echincea purpurea* (L.) Moench.	Asteraceae
Willow	*Salix alba* L.	Salicaceae
Goldenseal	*Hydrastis canadensis* L.	Ranunculaceae
Jewelweed	*Impatiens pallida* L.	Balsaminaceae
May apple	*Podophyllum peltatum* L.	Berberidaceae

based on any criteria deemed meaningful. After the first sort, consultants were asked to identify and explain each pile (e.g., edible greens, flowering herbs, etc.). Next, they were asked to group the most similar piles together (e.g., edible flowers with edible herbs, etc.) until only one pile remained. The 30 photos were then returned to their original piles, at which point the consultants were asked to divide them into smaller groups if possible (e.g., trees into fruit-bearing trees and nut-bearing trees, etc). Again, respondents were encouraged to elaborate on their sorting strategy upon completion of the task. When the pile sort was finished, a taxonomic "tree" of the resulting categories was drawn and discussed with the consultant in order to elicit and confirm which features they used to complete the sort (e.g., Furbee 1989).

THE CLASSIFICATION OF PLANTS

Multidimensional scaling was applied to the similarity matrices culled from the pile sort data. The contrast in sorting techniques of experts and novices is displayed in Figures 7.1 and 7.2. When the two plots are compared, some noteworthy differences emerge. As seen in the experts' sorts (Figure 7.1), plants are categorized according to a combination of attributes. An herbaceous-woody dimension runs from left to right across the plot. Leafy herbs

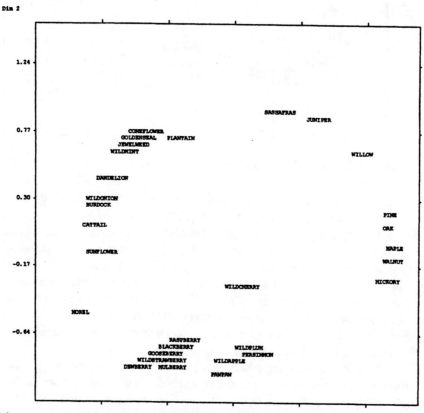

Figure 7.1. Multidimensional Scaling of Expert Pile Sorts

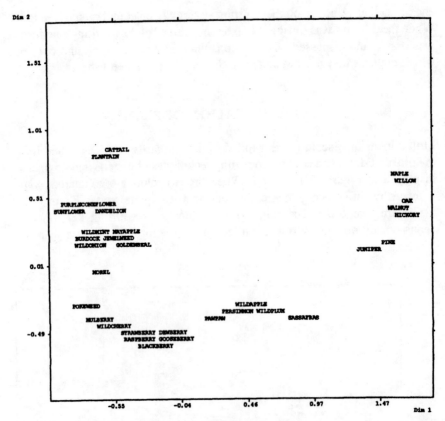

Figure 7.2.　Multidimensional Scaling of Novice Pile Sorts

and flowers occur on the left side of the figure (e.g., dandelion, wild onion, burdock) while trees appear on the right (e.g., willow, pine, oak). Along this dimension, the berry-producing shrubs are clustered toward the middle (e.g., blackberry, raspberry). Also evident is a culturally constructed, functional dimension of food to medicine, running vertically on Figure 7.1. Medicinal herbs and trees appear at the top (e.g., purple coneflower, plantain, sassafras, juniper) and the herbs and trees with edible parts occur toward the bottom (e.g., wild strawberry, persimmon, hickory). At the intersection of the two dimensions is wild cherry, a species with multiple uses, valued for its edibility, flavoring, and medicinal qualities.

For the novices, the scaling in Figure 7.2 reflects only one meaningful criteria of similarity—the visible distinction between woody species and herbaceous, leafy species. The general pattern here is rather similar to the experts', but without the "function" factor. The novice emphasizes perceptual cues and distinctive growth forms, as seen in the clusters of nut-bearing trees to the extreme right (e.g., oak, walnut, and hickory), and the pairing of cattail and plantain, both stalk-bearing species, on the upper left of the graph. Novices rely on morphology, a logical strategy, when categorizing plants. In so doing, novices tend to recognize scientifically related species and the families they constitute, such as the Asteraceae, represented here by dandelion, purple coneflower, and sunflower. Members of the Asteraceae share circular clusters of flowers with uniform centers and petal-shaped outer flowers. Also of interest is the pair between nut-bearing walnut and hickory (members of the family Juglandaceae), and the pairing of pine with juniper (members of the subdivision Pinacae). Interestingly, many of these associations were constructed covertly, without conscious recognition of their implications. For example, novices frequently explained that they were not quite certain why they sorted these items in the same pile, but that they simply "go together". The morel mushroom, sharing none of the qualities of the flower- or cone-bearing plants, appears by itself.

INTERPRETING THE PILE SORTS

At each stage of the successive sorting task, respondents were asked to describe the reasons behind their sorting decisions. Some 56% of the explanations cited by experts were linked to the use pattern, or activity context, of the plant. Experts described specific uses for groups of plants (e.g., "good choices in salads," "bases for spring tonics," or "excellent firewood"). Twenty nine percent of the experts' reasons were morphological, in which piles were labeled as "trees with soft wood," or "trees that lose their leaves." Eight percent of the reasons dealt with plant habitat or growth patterns (e.g., "these plants bear fruit in early summer") and the remaining 7% combined any of the above reasons together (e.g., "only the young shoots of these plants can be eaten," or "shrubs with sour-tasting berries"). By contrast, 79% of the explanations reported by novices were morphological, and usually based on simple features such as color (e.g., "herbs with small white flowers"), foliage (e.g., "trees with evergreen leaves"), or combinations of salient physical characteristics (e.g., "shrubby plants with clumps of berries"). Nine percent of the novices' sorting reasons were based on simple use patterns, usually ornamental (e.g., "these would make a nice table arrangement"). Covert features comprised 7% of the explanations (e.g., "I don't know, they just seem like brothers"). Finally, a lack of familiarity comprised the remaining 5% of the novices' explanations, including cases in which respondents were unable to classify the plants or had never encountered them before (e.g., "I've heard of these plants but I have no idea where they belong in these piles").

DIFFERENCES IN EXPERT AND NOVICE SORTING PATTERNS

To identify which species were sorted most differently by experts and novices, the aggregate respondent-by-plant matrix for the novices was subtracted from the aggregate matrix for the experts. In each of these matrices, the cell values represented the percentage of sorts in which two items were placed in the same pile. The matrix that resulted from the subtraction was converted to absolute values to reveal pairs of species that were sorted most differently by the two groups. Table 7.2 displays the seven pairs of plants with the highest percent difference in sorting similarity. Those species judged as similar by novices, but different by experts, include those with similar morphological attributes, such as sunflower and dandelion, and sassafras and pokeweed. Reasoning that these species share similar appearances (e.g., common flower shape, presence of berries), novices frequently sorted these species together, while experts did not. For experts, sassafras is considered a strong medicine, useful in the decoction of spring tonics, while pokeweed is valued as a salad food. On the other hand, experts frequently sorted wild onion and pokeweed together, deemed similar because they are commonly gathered and eaten together as wild greens in the springtime. Sharing few obvious visible similarities, these plants were judged as dissimilar by novices.

There are several pairs of plants that were classified similarly for both groups. The brambles, for example, which include blackberry, dewberry,

Table 7.2. Expert-Novice Differences in Sorting Strategies

Species pair		% Difference	Reason for grouping
Items grouped more frequently by experts than by novices			
Wild onion	Pokeweed	0.45	Cooked and eaten together
Wild mint	Purple coneflower	0.43	Used for spring tonics
Goldenseal	Sassafras	0.43	Used for spring tonics
Items grouped more frequently by novices than by experts			
Sunflower	Purple coneflower	0.57	Shape of flower
Sunflower	Dandelion	0.54	Shape of flower
Sassafras	Pokeweed	0.52	Color and shape of berries
Willow	Maple	0.51	Shape of leaves (willow) and fruits (maple)

raspberry, and others, were categorized together for experts and novices alike. However, this observation raises two important points: first, that form and function can be inherently related, as found among the edible berries, and second, that two groups may use different criteria even though they sort items similarly (e.g., Boster and Johnson 1989). For instance, experts explained the similarity between wild plum and wild apple in terms of their similar habitats and uses in pies and jellies; novices attributed their sameness to the common shape of their fruits. Further, while experts and novices each recognize a kinship between may apple, jewelweed and goldenseal, the experts sorted them on the basis of common medicinal properties, while novices classified them together because of the similarity in the color and pattern of their flowers. In sum, it appears that plants sharing common uses or applications are considered similar by experts, but not by novices; and plants with high perceptual affinity are judged similarly by novices, but not by experts.

CULTURAL CONSENSUS ANALYSIS

According to the cultural consensus model (Romney, Weller, and Batchelder 1986), the sharing of knowledge results in a higher level of agreement among those with experience, especially compared to individuals less informed about a given domain (e.g., novices). Using this model, it is thus possible to estimate the knowledge level, or "cultural competence" of each informant, based on his or her level of agreement with the aggregate or modal response. To determine whether or not a dataset fits the model, a minimum residual factor analysis is applied to an informant-by-informant correlation matrix. If the model holds, a single-factor solution should result, whereby no negative values appear on the first factor. Additionally, the largest eigenvalue should be substantially higher than the second and third (Romney 1999).

When cultural consensus analysis is applied to the combined group of experts and novices, the model fits the data. The scores on the first three eigenvalues are 8.029, 2.078, and 1.294, yielding a ratio of 3.864 between the first and second and 1.606 between the second and third. These results indicate that one single system of classification is shared by both novices and experts. However, when the two groups are separated, an interesting pattern emerges. The model fits nicely with the novice data, but not for the experts'. Moreover, a higher mean cultural competence value was found for the novices ($M = .644$, s.d. $= .102$) than the experts ($M = .496$, s.d. $= .237$). This difference is statistically significant (t $= 1.80$, p $< .05$).

Multidimensional scaling was applied to the aggregate informant-by-informant correlation matrix, as shown by Figure 7.3. As seen in the scaling, the

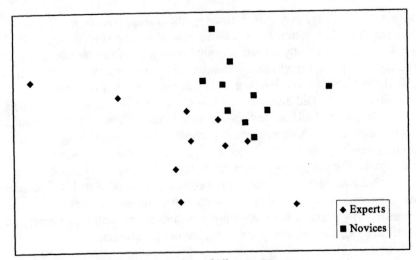

Figure 7.3. Multidimensional Scaling of Pile Sort Responses

novices are clustered more closely to one another than the experts, who are in general more widely dispersed. This configuration suggests that while novices and experts generally form their own respective groupings, the "core" cluster for the entire respondent set is comprised of both experts *and* novices. Accordingly, one single classification system exists.

Similar results are reported by Boster and Johnson (1989), who used pile sorts to examine the similarity judgements of marine fish among expert fishermen and a novice control group. The authors proffer the following explanation for the relative absence of agreement observed among their experts:

> Because experts control more different kinds of knowledge and offer more varied justifications for their responses than do novices, they might be expected to be more variable in their responses than the novices (Boster and Johnson 1989:877).

The results reported in the present study support the notion that experts command a greater diversity of information regarding the ecological role and practical, cultural value of wild flora, which in turn provides them with more alternatives when "constructing" taxonomies. As interest and skill increases with respect to a semantic domain, the scope of information becomes increasingly varied (e.g., Medin et al. 1997). Cognitive anthropologists have noted that the acquisition of expertise entails a movement from imagistic recognition to more abstract, esoteric discrimination strategies (e.g., Kempton 1981, Chick and Roberts 1987). This progression has been reported in a number of studies ranging from expert-novice categorization of physics problems (Chi, Feltovich, and Glaser 1981) and X-ray pictures (Lesgold et al. 1988), to the differences in classification of wine (Solomon 1997) and art (Hekkert and Van Wieringen 1997).

STRUCTURAL DIFFERENCES IN
EXPERT AND NOVICE TAXONOMIES

In order to examine more closely the variance in plant classification, the two experts and two novices whose responses scored highest for competency were selected for discussion. The experts' taxonomies appear in Figures 7.4a and 7.4b, and the novices' are given in Figures 7.5a and 7.5b. Even the most typical "modal" expert respondents use markedly different combinations of features when generating taxonomic models. For Expert "A", the labels assigned to the terminal categories reflect an emphasis on subtle, functional values of plants (e.g., strong vs. weak medicinals, high vs. low quality in edibility). For Expert "B", however, the labeling pattern suggests an attention to specific use contexts (e.g., salad greens, beverage plants, desserts). By contrast, much less variation is seen between the two novices (Figures 7.5a and 7.5b). The novice

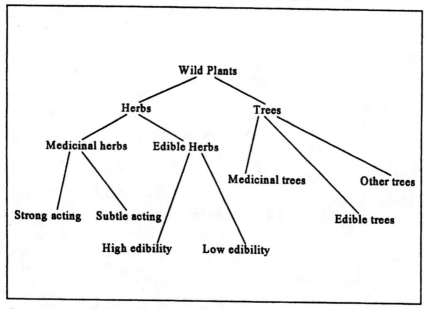

Figure 7.4a.   Taxonomic Tree for Expert "A"

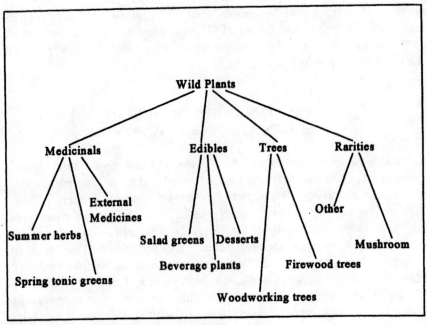

Figure 7.4b. Taxonomic Tree for Expert "B"

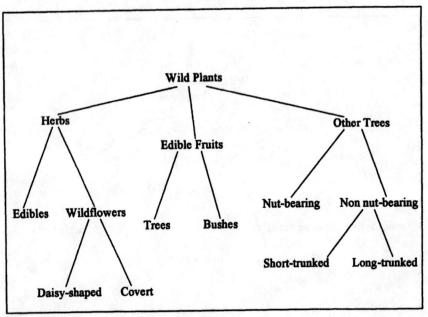

Figure 7.5a. Taxonomic Tree for Novice "A"

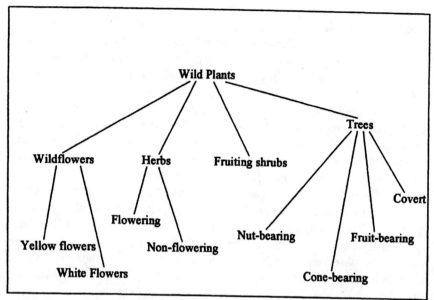

Figure 7.5b. Taxonomic Tree for Novice "B"

taxonomies are based primarily on the distribution and occurrence of specific morphological traits (e.g., white vs. yellow flowers; fruit-, nut-, and cone-bearing trees). The reliance on limited sets of perceptible features probably explains the higher similarity scores in the novices' pile sort responses. The differences observed in the experts' taxonomies reflect a more expansive range of knowledge and a more complex and variable combination of descriptive utilitarian features used to construct meaningful categories of useful flora.

In an effort to delve deeper into the hierarchical nature of plant classification, the total set of expert and novice taxonomies was compared for this study (cf. Medin et al. 1997). Two compelling differences were found regarding the width and depth of experts' and novices' taxonomies. First, the experts averaged more initial piles (5.8) on their first sort than novices (3.6), a difference with statistical significance ($t = 3.08$, $p < .01$). Secondly, and somewhat unexpectedly, the novices averaged a greater number of taxonomic levels (3.6) than the experts (2.4), a difference that is also significant ($t = 2.45$, $p < .05$). These data yield important insights into the cognitive structure of ethnobotanical systems. Experts generated broader taxonomies with a high number of initial groupings but with fewer higher-order specific categories. On the other hand, novices produced narrower taxonomies, but somewhat deeper with highly inclusive initial classes and many higher-order subgroups. By focusing primarily on the dispersal of morphological traits, novices generate the kind of structural depth often associated with scientific, phylogenetic arrangements (e.g., Medin et al. 1997). Conversely, by differentiating between use categories early on in the classification procedure, experts offered broad, shallow hierarchies typically found in folk taxonomies of cultural domains (e.g., Furbee 1989, Berlin 1992).

The apparent shift from simple to complex classification strategies probably explains why the experts show less intra-group agreement than the novices, who are logically restricted to perceptual attributes. One rather unexpected outcome was a higher level of agreement among novices, which according to the consensus model, could be taken as evidence of cultural competence. These findings, then, urge a word of caution for future researchers who could misinterpret patterns of intra-group agreement as evidence for domain expertise. Simply put, agreement may reflect a shared, albeit simplistic and imagistic style of classifying things into groups that "make sense" to the more casual observer. Though agreement is characteristic among experts, it can also indicate a common naivete, or knowledge gap, among the less informed.

CHAPTER SUMMARY

This chapter presents the results to the pile sort task, designed to elicit the structure of ethnobotanical classification systems of experts and novices in Little Dixie. As expected, it is shown that experts base their similarity judgements on a combination of utilitarian and morphological attributes, while novices rely generally on easily observed form features. Contrary to the hypothesis, however, a single classification system underlies the responses of experts and novices. When all respondents are examined as a combined group, the core cluster of highly competent individuals is comprised of both experts and novices. Further, novices show a higher level of consensus among themselves than experts, who agree less among themselves because they have more knowledge of alternative ways of categorizing the plants that populate the fertile fields and forests of Little Dixie.

Chapter Eight

Conclusion

The chapters of this book have aimed to describe one aspect of cultural knowledge in Missouri's Little Dixie. Indeed, *what* and *how* people come to know about wild botanicals is a complex and multi-faceted topic, primarily because people have different ways of envisioning and using plants in their daily lives (Logan and Dixon 1994). Further, plants have varying levels of functional and symbolic meaning for members of all societies. Through the lens of ethnobotany, these pages intend to convey a deeper understanding of the perceptual, cognitive, and cultural factors that shape human acquisition and application of wild plant knowledge, and a sense of how regional flora are understood as sustainable natural resources. Beyond the insights about people-plants relationships, ethnobotany generates understandings of rural life in the US, which in turn illuminates how rural culture is understood by others.

Ethnobotanical knowledge in Little Dixie is not static, nor is it acquired randomly. Rather, it is a dynamic process under constant modification and revision as years go by. Age-old traditions of plant use in Little Dixie have cultural origins in Southern Appalachia and the British Isles, and others have historic ties to the customs of Native American peoples. And a good deal of surviving plant knowledge stems from continued innovation and experimentation with native flora. The perceptual and sensory appeal of plants is the principal factor attracting humans in the first place. All evidence indicates that a limited number of plant families with considerable use potential are used more frequently and consistently than others. These results substantiate the notion that human recognition of plants is a selective and systematic process, leading ultimately to interaction with culturally valuable species. Families with high use value include the fruits and berries of the rose family

(Rosaceae), numerous members of the bean family (Fabaceae), and the widespread, brightly flowered members of the sunflower family (Asteraceae).

Experts of cultural domains maintain more abstract, complex, culturally-guided conceptions of those domains. As expected, the experts in this study maintain a larger and more functionally elaborate knowledge system. Here, experts differ from others by virtue of the types of plants they know, and their particular mode of use. Specifically, experts offered more esoteric information about plants (e.g., the medicinal benefits of herbs and roots). Novices use plants in more exoteric ways. Experts are also more cognizant of species that do not grow locally in their home counties. These data suggest that all people, experts and novices alike, are most aware of species that are readily accessible to them. In Little Dixie, culture and ecology are inextricably linked. Residents of Little Dixie are connected to their living landscapes in a number of cognitive and emotional ways.

Further, it was shown that experts combine features of form (e.g., color) and function (e.g., food) in the classification of plants, while novices rely generally on form. Experts categorize plants according to shared uses or common applications, while novices consider plants with high perceptual affinity to be more fundamentally related. Even though experts and novices clearly approach classification in different ways, the cultural consensus model reveals a cohesive, shared categorization system. These results could indicate that the consensus model is reflecting a shared pattern by which experts and novices both rely on morphological attributes when constructing their taxonomies. It is conceivable that human recognition and categorization operate in fundamentally similar ways for all ethnobiological domains—birds, trees, fishes, and so forth. The accumulation of knowledge appears to generate alternative information processing strategies. Experience and learning trigger a cognitive shift from the assimilation of perceptual attributes to the integration of functional attributes. It should be noted, however, that perceptual and cognitive processing are not mutually exclusive. In the gradual shift from naivete to expertise, the perceptual model is built upon—but not entirely replaced—by the functional model.

As a cultural practice shared among so many Little Dixie residents, wild plant procurement remains, most importantly, a socially meaningful and revivifying activity. The importance of natural resource procurement to cultural identity has been well documented by folklorists and anthropologists (e.g., Gillespie 1984, Gutierrez 1984, Marshall 1974). Here it has been shown that gathering, using, and understanding wild plants is inexorably tied to one's sense of place in Little Dixie. In his discussion of regional folkways in the United States, Tuleja posits that local traditions are much more than mere relics of nostalgia. They may represent a strategy of resistance to cultural homogenization:

. . .to embrace an ethnic or regional style becomes, far more than a quirk of identity, a centrifugal empowerment. In their zest for the particular, the actors here enlist "survivals" in a quest for personal communion, for collective identity—and for survival itself (1997:15).

Wild plant procurement, wherever it occurs, is at once a creative and functional response to the need to sustain regional cohesion in a globalizing world.

While the preservation of local knowledge is crucial to sustaining biodiversity, ethnobotanists must continue to explore the relations between ecology, culture, and human cognition. The extent to which cultural knowledge mirrors the ecological characteristics of a region varies from place to place. But in Little Dixie, tradition and environment are intimately connected, despite the slow burn of urban encroachment. Purposeful inquiry into human ecological relations, in the United States and beyond, is critical for survival not only in the ethnobotanical sense, but for the cultural well-being of present generations and those yet to follow.

Appendix

Composite Inventory of Free-Listed Species and their Reported Uses

Appendix

Vernacular name	Scientific name	Uses for plant	Part of Plant Used
Alum root	*Heuchera americana* L.	medicine	roots
Amaranth	*Amaranthus* L. spp.	food	leaves, seeds
Apple	*Malus pumila* Mill.	food, wood	fruits, whole tree
Ash	*Fraxinus americana* L.	wood	trunk
Asparagus	*Asparagus officinalis* L.	food, tea	whole plant, leaves, seeds
Aster	*Aster* L. spp.	ornamental	flowers
Basswood	*Tilia americana* L.	lumber	wood
Bayberry	*Myrica* L. spp.	crafts, making candles	leaves, berries
Beebalm	*Monarda didyma* L.	ornamental, wildlife forage	all
Beggars lice	*Lappula echinata* Gilib.	wildlife forage, fix nitrogen in soil	plant, seeds
Big Bluestem	*Andropogon gerardii* Vitman.	wildlife forage	plant
Birch	*Betula* L. spp.	lumber, shade	wood, all
Bittersweet	*Solanum dulcamara* L.	ornamental	whole plant (not roots)
Black cohosh	*Cimicifuga racemosa* (L.) Nutt.	medicine	bark
Black haw	*Viburnum prunifolium* L.	medicine	roots
Black locust	*Robinia pseudo-acacia* L.	lumber	wood
Blackberry	*Rubus* L. spp.	food, medicine, wildlife forage, tea	berries, roots, fruits, leaves
Blackeyed susan	*Rudbeckia hirta* L.	ornamental, flower gardens	flowers, whole flower, plant
Blazing star	*Liatris* Schreb. spp.	ornamental	plant
Bloodroot	*Sanguinaria canadensis* L.	medicine	root
Blue cohosh	*Caulophyllum thalictroides* (L.) Michx.	medicine	roots
Bluebells	*Mertensia virginica* (L.) Pers.	ornamental	whole
Bluestem	*Andropogon virginicus* L.	wildlife forage	whole plant
Boneset	*Eupatorium perfoliatum* L.	medicine	leaves
Burdock	*Arctium minus* Bernh.	food, medicine, blood purifier	leaves, roots
Burhead	*Echniodorus cordifolius* (L.) Griseb.	wildlife forage	seeds
Butterfly weed	*Asclepias tuberosa* L.	wildlife forage	plant
Cardinal flower	*Lobelia cardinalis* L.	water gardens, wildlife forage	all
Carpenters square	*Scrophularia marilandica* L.	medicine, food	leaves, greens
Catnip	*Nepeta cataria* L.	cat tonic	leaves
Cattail	*Typha latifolia* L.	food, ornamental, sewage treatment	rootstock, stalk, seed head

Chamomile	*Matricaria chamomila* L.	sedative tea, medicine	flowers
Chestnut	*Castanea dentata* (Marsh.) Borkh.	food	nuts
Chickweed	*Stellaria media* L.	medicine, food	leaves, stems, greens, blossoms
Chicory	*Cichorium intybus* L.	food, tea	roots, leaves, flowers
Chokecherry	*Prunus virginiana* L.	medicine	berries, bark
Chufa	*Cyperus esculentus* L.	wildlife forage	seeds
Cleavers	*Galium aparine* L.	medicine	stalk, leaves
Clover	*Trifolium repens* L.	wildlife forage, nitrogen fixing	whole plant
Coltsfoot	*Petasites hybridus* L.	medicine	leaf stem
Columbine	*Aquilegia canadensis* L.	ornamental	flowers
Coreopsis	*Coreopsis tinctoria* Nutt.	flower gardens	plants
Cornflower	*Centaurea cyanus* L.	ornamental	flowers
Cottonwood	*Populus deltoides* Marsh.	lumber	trunk
Cow parsnip	*Heracleum lanatum* Michx.	food	leaves
Crabapple	*Pyrus* L. spp.	food	fruits
Crabgrass	*Digitaria* Heist. spp.	ground cover	all
Currant	*Ribes odoratum* Wendl.	food	berries
Cypress	*Taxodium distichum* (L.) Rich.	lumber	wood
Daisy	*Chrysanthemum leucanthemum* L.	ornamental	flowers
Dandelion	*Taraxacum officinale* Weber.	food, medicine, wildlife forage	flowers, leaves
Daylily	*Hemerocallis fulva* L.	ornamental	flowers
Dewberry	*Rubus flagellaris* Willd.	food, wildlife forage	berries, fruits
Dill	*Anethum graveolens* L.	food, pickling	tops
Dogwood	*Cornus florida* L.	ornamental	whole
Duckweed	*Spirodela* Schleiden spp.	aquatic protection	all
Elderberry	*Sambucus canadensis* L.	food, medicine	berries
Ferns	*Polypodium* (Tourn.) L. spp.	food, ornamental	crowns
Fescue grass	*Festuca* L. spp.	food for cattle	stems, leaves
Feverfew	*Chrysanthemum parthenium* (L.) Bernh.	medicine	leaves
Foxglove	*Digitalis purpurea* L.	medicine	flowers, leaves
Gentian	*Gentiana quinquefolia* L.	medicine	roots, leaves
Ginseng	*Panax quinquefolius* L.	medicine, stimulant	roots
Goats rue	*Tephrosia virginiana* (L.) Pers.	fish bait	plant

(continued)

Vernacular name	Scientific name	Uses for plant	Part of Plant Used
Goldenrod	Solidago L. spp.	wildlife forage	blossom
Goldenseal	Hydrastis canadensis L.	medicine, blood purifier	roots, leaves, plant
Gooseberry	Ribes missouriense Nutt.	food, forage	fruits, berries
Grass	various species of Poaceae	wildlife forage, stop erosion	stalk, leaves
Hawthorn	Crataegus L. spp.	medicine	roots
Hazelnut	Corylus L. spp.	wildlife forage, ornamental, food	whole plant, nuts
Hemlock	Cicuta maculata L.	poison	leaves
Hemp	Cannabis sativa L.	medicine, crafts, paper products	leaves, stalks, buds, fibers
Hickory	Carya Nutt. spp.	food, forage, lumber, crafts	nuts, wood, trunk, bark
Holly	Ilex opaca Ait.	ornamental	all, berries, leaves
Horehound	Marrubium vulgare L.	medicine	leaves
Horsetail	Equisetum arvense L.	scouring pads, musical instruments	stems, stalk
Huckleberry	Gaylussacia baccata (Wang.) K. Koch.	food	berries
Hyssop	Hyssopus officinalis L.	cleaning	leaves
Indian grass	Sorghastrum nutans (L.) Nash	wildlife forage	plant
Indian paintbrush	Castilleja coccinea (L.) K. Spreng.	ornamental, flower gardens	flowers, plant
Indigo	Baptisia Vent. spp.	crafts, fix nitrogen in soil	plant
Iris	Iris L. spp.	wildlife forage, ornamental	plant, all, root
Jack in the pulpit	Arisaema triphyllum (L.) Schott.	ornamental	whole plant
Jewelweed	Impatiens pallida L.	medicine, poison ivy	leaves, stems
Joe Pye weed	Eupatorium purpureum L.	medicine, spring tonic	leaves, roots
Juniper	Juniperus virginiana L.	medicine, ornamental, food, windbreak	berries, whole tree
Ladyslipper	Cypripedium L. spp.	ornamental	flowers
Lambsquarters	Chenopodium album L.	food, greens, purifier	leaves
Larkspur	Delphinium L. spp.	ornamental	whole
Lead plant	Amorpha canescens Pursh.	fix nitrogen in soil	plant
Lespedeza	Lespedeza Michx. spp.	fix nitrogen in soil	plant
Licorice	Glycyrrhiza lepidota (Nutt.) Pursh	food	roots
Lilac	Syringa vulgaris L.	ornamental	flower
Little Bluestem	Andropogon L. spp.	wildlife forage	plant
Maple	Acer saccharum L.	lumber, ornamental, food, shade	wood, whole tree, sap, trunk
Marijuana	Cannabis sativa L.	clothing, smoking, medicine	leaf, buds
May apple	Podophyllum peltatum L.	medicine, food	fruits

Milkweed	Asclepias syriaca L.	medicine, wildlife forage	milk, pod, leaves
Miner's lettuce	Lactuca L. spp.	food	leaves, greens
Morel	Morchella esculenta L.	food, medicine	whole mushroom, tops
Mugwort	Artemisia vulgaris L.	insect repellent	leaves
Mulberry	Morus rubra L.	food, medicine, shade	fruits, berries
Mullein	Verbascum thapsus L.	ornamental, medicine, toilet paper	whole plant, leaves
Mustard	Brassica L. spp.	food	seeds
Nettles	Urtica L. spp.	crafts, medicine, food	leaves, fruit, greens
Ninebark	Physocarpus opulifolius L.	stabilize stream bank, medicine	whole plant, inner bark
Oak	Quercus L. spp.	lumber, crafts, forage, firewood, shade	wood, acorns, trunk, nuts
Ohio buckeye	Aesculus hippocastanum L.	good luck piece	nuts, wood
Osage orange	Maclura pomifera (Raf.) Schneid.	firewood, moth repellent	wood, fruit
Passionflower	Passiflora incarnata L.	medicine	leaves
Paw paw	Asimina triloba (L.) Dunal	food	fruits
Peach	Prunus persica L.	food	fruits
Pear	Pyrus communis L.	food	fruits
Pecan	Carya illinoensis (Wang.) K. Koch.	food, wood	nuts, wood
Pencil flower	Stylosanthes biflora (L.) BSP.	fix nitrogen in soil	plant
Pennyroyal	Hedeoma pulegioides (L.) Pers.	tea, medicine	leaves
Persimmon	Diospyros virginiana L.	food	fruits, seeds
Pickerel weed	Pontederia cordata L.	water gardens, wildlife forage	plant
Pine	Pinus echinata L.	lumber, ornamental, shade, food	wood, trunk, cones, needles
Plantain	Plantago major L.	medicine, food	leaves, roots, flowers, all
Pokeweed	Phytolacca americana L.	food, crafts, medicine	leaves, berries, greens
Poppy	Argemone albiflora Hornem	food	seeds
Prairie cordgrass	Spartina pectinata Link	stabilize stream bank	plant
Prairie dropseed	Sporobolus heterolepis (Gray) Gray	wildlife forage	plant
Prickly pear	Opuntia humifusa (Raf.) Raf	food	leaves, fruits, flowers
Primrose	Oenothera biennis L.	flower gardens, food, medicine	plant, oil
Purple coneflower	Echincea purpurea (L.) Moench.	medicine, wildlife forage	leaves, roots, flowers, all
Purslane	Portulaca oleracea L.	food	greens, leaves
Pussywillow	Salix humilis Marsh.	ornamental	stems
Queen Anne's lace	Daucus carota L.	attracting insects, wildlife forage	flowers, leaves

(continued)

Vernacular name	Scientific name	Uses for plant	Part of Plant Used
Quinine	Parthenium integrifolium L.	medicine	roots, leaves
Raspberry	Rubus strigosus Michx.	food, medicine	berries, roots, leaves, fruit
Rattlebox	Crotolaria L. spp.	fix nitrogen in soil	plant
Rattlesnake master	Eryngium yuccifolium Michx.	crafts	leaves
Red clover	Trifolium pratense L.	wildlife forage, medicine	flowers, leaves
Redbud	Cercis canadensis L.	ornamental, shade	whole plant
Royal catchfly	Silene regia Sims.	flower gardens	plant
Sarsaparilla	Aralia nudicaulis L.	food	leaves
Sassafras	Sassafras albidum (Nutt.) Nees.	food, medicine, tea, lumber	roots, bark, trunk, leaves
Senna	Cassia marilandica L.	medicine	leaves
Shadbush	Amelanchier arborea (Michx. f.) Fern.	ornamental	whole plant
Sheep sorrel	Rumex acetosella L.	food	leaves
Shepards purse	Capsella bursa-pastoris (L.) Medic.	medicine	leaves, stem
Shooting stars	Dodecatheon meadia L.	ornamental	plant
Slippery elm	Ulmus rubra Muhl	medicine	bark
Smartweed	Polygonum L. spp.	wildlife forage	seeds
Snakeroot	Eupatorium rugosum Houtt.	medicine, treatment for snakebite	root
Snow on the mountain	Euphorbia marginata Pursh.	ornamental	plant
Solomons seal	Polygonatum Mill. spp.	medicine	leaves
Sorrel	Rumex L. spp.	food	leaves
Spearmint	Mentha spicata L.	food, tea	leaves
Spiderwort	Tradescantia subaspera Ker.	ornamental	whole plant
Sumac	Rhus L. spp.	medicine, spring tonic	berries, bark, fruit
Sunflower	Helianthus annuus L.	food, ornamental, wildlife forage	seeds, whole flower, plant
Sweet clover	Melilotus alba Medic.	wildlife forage	nectar
Sweet William	Phlox divaricata L.	ornamental	whole plant
Switch grass	Panicum virgatum L.	wildlife forage, levee stabilizer	plant
Sycamore	Platanus occidentalis L.	lumber	trunk
Tansy	Tanacetum vulgare L.	insect repellent	flower, leaves
Teasel	Dipsacus sylvestris Huds.	ornamental	head, stem
Trumpet vine	Campsis radicans (L.) Seem.	ornamental	all
Violet	Viola L. spp.	ornamental, medicine, food, perfume	leaves, flowers, greens, blossoms
Walnut	Juglans L. spp.	food, medicine, poison, firewood, forage	nuts, hulls, bark, wood

Watercress	*Nasturtium officinale* R. Br.	medicine, food	leaves, greens, blossoms
Waterlilly	*Nymphaea odorata* Ait.	ornamental	all
Weeping willow	*Salix babylonica* L.	shade	whole tree
White clover	*Trifolium repens* L.	fix nitrogen in soil	plant
White sage	*Artemisia ludoviciana* Nutt.	medicine	leaves
Wild cherry	*Prunus serotina* Ehrh.	food, medicine, lumber	berries, bark, fruit
Wild chervil	*Anthriscus cerefolium* (L.) Hoffm.	food, garnish	stems, leaves
Wild garlic	*Allium canadense* L.	food	bulb
Wild ginger	*Asarum canadense* L.	medicine	roots
Wild grape	*Vitis* L. spp.	food, wine, ornamental	fruits, vines
Wild mint	*Mentha arvensis* L.	food, medicine, tea	leaves
Wild oats	*Uvularia sessilifolia* L.	food	grain
Wild onion	*Allium stellatum* Ker.	food, medicine, blood purifier	bulb, roots, leaves, stalk
Wild parsnip	*Pastinaca sativa* L.	food	roots
Wild plum	*Prunus americana* L.	food	fruits
Wild rose	*Rosa* L. spp.	food	berries
Wild strawberry	*Fragaria virginiana* L.	food	berries, fruits
Willow	*Salix alba* L.	medicine, crafts, ornamental, food	bark, whole tree, stalks, leaves
Winter cress	*Barbarea vulgaris* R. Brown	food	greens
Yarrow	*Achillea millefolium* L.	medicine	leaf stem, flowers
Yellow dock	*Rumex crispus* L.	blood purifier, medicine	roots, bark, leaves

Bibliography

Alcorn, Janice B. 1995a. The Scope and Aims of Ethnobotany in a Developing World. Pp. 23–39 in *Ethnobotany: Evolution of a Discipline*, edited by Richard Evans Schultes and Siri Von Reis. Dioscorides Press, Portland.

———. 1995b. Ethnobotanical Knowledge Systems: A Resource for Meeting Rural Development Goals. Pp. 1–12 in *The Cultural Dimension of Development: Indigenous Knowledge Systems*, edited by D. Michael Warren, L. Jan Slikkerveer, and David Brokensha. Intermediate Technology Publications, London.

——— 1981. Factors Influencing Resource Perception Among the Huastec: Suggestions for Future Ethnobotanical Inquiry. *Journal of Ethnobiology* 1(2):221–230

Balée, William. 1999. Footprints of the Forest: Ka'apor Ethnobotany–The Historical Ecology of Plant Utilization by an Amazonian People. Columbia University Press, New York.

Balick, Michael. 1996. Ethnobotany: Linking Health and Environmental Conservation. Pp. 201–9 in *The Ecology of Health: Identifying Issues and Alternatives*, edited by Jennifer Chesworth. Sage Publications, Thousand Oaks, CA.

Benz, Bruce F., Francisco Santana M., Rosario Pineda L., Judith Cevallos E., Luis Robles H., Domitila de Niz L. 1994. Characterization of Mestizo Plant Use in the Sierra de Manantlan, Jalisco-Colima, Mexico. *Journal of Ethnobiology* 14(1):23–42.

Berlin, Brent. 1992. *Ethnobiological Classification: Principles of Categorization of Plants and Animals in Traditional Societies*. Princeton University Press, Princeton.

———. 1972. Speculations of the Growth of Ethnobotanical Nomenclature. *Language in Society* 1:51–86.

Berlin, Elois Ann and Brent Berlin. 1996. *Medical Ethnobotany of the Highland Maya of Chiapas, Mexico*. Princeton University Press, Princeton.

Bernard, H. Russell. 1994. *Research Methods in Anthropology*. Sage Publications, Thousand Oaks, CA.

Borgatti, Stephen P. 1995. ANTHROPAC 4.95. Analytic Technologies, Columbia, SC.

Boster, James. 1994. The Successive Pile Sort. *Cultural Anthropology Methods* 6:11–12.

Boster, James S. and Jeffrey C. Johnson. 1989. Form or Function: A Comparison of Expert and Novice Judgments of Similarity Among Fish. *American Anthropologist* 91:866–889.

Boster, James, Brent Berlin, and John P. O'Neill. 1986. The Correspondence of Jivoran to Scientific Ornithology. *American Anthropologist* 88(3):569–583.

Brady, Erika. 1990. Mankind's Thumb on Nature's Scale: Trapping and Regional Identity in the Missouri Ozarks. Pp. 58–73 in *Sense of Place: American Regional Cultures*, edited by Barbara Allen and Thomas J. Schlereth. The University Press of Kentucky, Lexington.

Brown, Cecil H. 1985. Mode of Subsistence and Folk Biological Taxonomy. *Current Anthropology* 27:1–18.

———. 1979. Folk Zoological Life-Forms: Their Universality and Growth. *American Anthropologist* 81(4):791–817.

———. 1977. Folk Botanical Life-Forms: Their Universality and Growth. *American Anthropologist* 79(2):317–342.

Browner, Carole H. 1985. Criteria for Selecting Herbal Remedies. *Ethnology* 24:13–32.

Caniago, Izefri and Stephen F. Siebert. 1998. Medicinal Plant Ecology, Knowledge, and Conservation in Kalimantan, Indonesia. *Economic Botany* 52(3):229–250.

Casagrande, David G. 2000. Human Taste and Cognition in Tzeltal Maya Medicinal Plant Use. *Journal of Ecological Anthropology* 4:57–69

Chi, M. T. H., Feltovich, P. J., and Glaser, R. 1981. Categorization and Representation of Physics Problems by Experts and Novices. *Cognitive Science* 5:121–152.

Chick, Garry and John M. Roberts. 1987. Lathe Craft: A Study in "Part" Appreciation. *Human Organization* 46(4):305–317.

Christensen, Lawrence O. 1990. Missouri: The Heart of the Nation. Pp. 86–106 in *Heartland: Comparative Histories of the Midwestern States,* edited by James H. Madison. Indiana University Press, Bloomington.

Coffey, Timothy. 1993. *The History and Folklore of North American Wildflowers.* Facts on File, New York.

Conklin, Harold C. 1954. An Ethnoecological Approach to Shifting Agriculture. *Transactions of the New York Academy of Sciences* 17:133–142.

Cotton, C. M. 1996. *Ethnobotany: Principles and Applications.* John Wiley and Sons, Chichester, England.

Crisler, Robert M. 1948. Missouri's Little Dixie. *Missouri Historical Review* 42:130–139.

Danielson, Larry. 1990. Tornado Stories in the Breadbasket: Weather and Regional Identity. Pp. 28–39 in *Sense of Place: American Regional Cultures*, edited by Barbara Allen and Thomas J. Schlereth. The University Press of Kentucky, Lexington.

Elizabetsky, E. and P. Shanley. 1994. Ethnopharmacology in the Brazilian Amazon. *Pharmacology and Therapeutics* 64:201–214.

Estabrook, George F. 1994. Choice of Fuel for Bagaco Still Helps Maintain Biological Diversity in a Traditional Portuguese Agricultural System. *Journal of Ethnobiology* 14(1):43–58.

Etkin, Nina L. 1990. Ethnopharmacology: Biological and Behavioral Perspectives in the Study of Indigenous Medicines. Pp. 149–158 in *Medical Anthropology: Contemporary Theory and Method*, edited by Thomas M. Johnson and Carolyn F. Sargent. Praeger, New York.

Flannery, Kent (editor). 1986. *Guila Naquitz: Archaic Foraging and Early Agriculture in Oaxaca, Mexico*. Academic Press, Orlando.

Foster, Steven and James A. Duke. 1990. *A Field Guide to Medicinal Plants: Eastern and Central North America*. Houghton Mifflin, Boston.

Freethy, Ron. 1985. *From Agar to Zenry: A Book of Plant Uses, Names, and Folklore*. Tanager Books, Dover, NH.

Freudenberg, William R. 1986. The Density of Acquaintanceship: An Overlooked Variable in Community Research? *American Journal of Sociology* 92:27–63.

Furbee, Louanna. 1989. A Folk Expert System: Soils Classification in the Colca Valley, Peru. *Anthropological Quarterly* 29:83–102.

Garro, Linda. 1986. Intracultural Variation in Folk Medical Knowledge: A Comparison Between Curers and Non-Curers. *American Anthropologist* 88:351–370.

Gemeinhardt, Todd R., Justin M. Nolan, Douglas B. Noltie, and Michael C. Robbins. 2001. Fishing for Ideas: Teaching and Learning in a University Ichthyology Course. *Fisheries* 26(12):6–14.

Gibbens, Byrd. 1992. Customs and Beliefs. Pp. 155–172 *in An Arkansas Folklore Sourcebook*, edited by W. K.McNeil and William M. Clements. University of Arkansas Press, Fayetteville.

Gillespie, Angus K. 1984. A Wilderness in the Megalopolis: Foodways in the Pine Barrens of New Jersey. Pp. 145–168 in *Ethnic and Regional Foodways in the United States*, edited by Linda Keller Brown and Kay Mussell. The University of Tennessee Press, Knoxville.

Gregory, Cecil L. 1958. *Rural Social Areas in Missouri*. The University of Missouri Agricultural Experiment Station Research Bulletin no. 665. The University of Missouri, Columbia.

Gutierrez, C. Paige. 1984. The Social and Symbolic Uses of Ethnic/Regional Foodways: Cajuns and Crawfish in South Louisiana. Pp. 169–184 in *Ethnic and Regional Foodways in the United States*, edited by Linda Keller Brown and Kay Mussell. The University of Tennessee Press, Knoxville.

Hatfield, Gabrielle. 1994. *Country Remedies: Traditional East Anglian Plant Remedies in the Twentieth Century*. The Boydell Press, Woodbridge, England.

Hekkert, Paul and Piet C. W. Van Wieringen. 1996. Beauty in the Eye of Expert and Nonexpert Beholders: A Study in the Appraisal of Art. *American Journal of Psychology* 109(3):389–407.

Henley, Nancy M. 1969. A Psychological Study of the Semantics of Animal Terms. *Journal of Verbal Learning and Verbal Behavior* 8:176–184.

Holman, Eric W. 2005. Domain-Specific and General Properties of Folk Classifications. *Journal of Ethnobiology* 25(1):71–92.

Holmes, Walter C. 1990. *Flore Louisiana: An Ethno-botanical Study of French-Speaking Louisiana*. University of Southwestern Louisiana Press, Lafayette.

Hunn, Eugene. 1982. The Utilitarian Factor in Folk Biological Classification. *American Anthropologist* 84:830–847.

Hunter, Carl G. 1989. *Trees, Shrubs, and Vines of Arkansas.* The Ozark Society Foundation, Little Rock.

——. 1984. *Wildflowers of Arkansas.* The Ozark Society Foundation and Arkansas Game and Fish Commission, Little Rock.

Hurt, R. Douglas. 1992. *Agriculture and Slavery in Missouri's Little Dixie.* University of Missouri Press, Columbia.

Janiskee, Robert L. 1991. Rural Festivals in South Carolina. *Journal of Cultural Geography* 11(2):31–43.

——. 1980. South Carolina's Harvest Festivals: Rural Delights for Day Tripping Urbanites. *Journal of Cultural Geography* 1(1):96–104.

Johns, Timothy. 1996. *The Origins of Human Diet and Medicine.* University of Arizona Press, Tucson.

——. 1994. Ambivalence to the Palatability Factors in Wild Food Plants. Pp. 46–61 in *Eating on the Wild Side,* edited by Nina L. Etkin. The University of Arizona Press, Tucson.

Jones, Timothy. 2000. Commentary on "Cultural Conservation of Medicinal Plant Use in the Ozarks." *Human Organization* 59(1):136–140.

Kay, Jeanne. 1982. The Ecological Basis of Menominee Ethnobotany. *Journal of Cultural Geography* 2(2):1–12.

Kaye, Connie and Neil Billington. 1997. *Medicinal Plants of the Heartland.* Cache River Press, Vienna, IL.

Kempton, Willett. 1981. *The Folk Classification of Ceramics: A Study of Cognitive Prototypes.* Academic Press, New York.

Kindscher, Kelly. 1992. *Medicinal Wild Plants of the Prairie: An Ethnobotanical Guide.* University Press of Kansas, Lawrence.

——. 1987. *Edible Wild Plants of the Prairie: An Ethnobotanical Guide.* University Press of Kansas, Lawrence.

Koch, William E. 1980. *Folklore from Kansas: Customs, Beliefs, and Superstitions.* Regents Press of Kansas, Lawrence.

Krochmal, Arnold and Connie Krochmal. 1984. *A Field Guide to Medicinal Plants.* Times Books, New York.

Lesgold, Alan, Harriet Rubinson, Paul Feltovich, Robert Glaser, Dale Klopfer, and Yen Wang. 1988. Expertise in a Complex Skill: Diagnosing X-Ray Pictures. Pp. 311–313 in *The Nature of Expertise,* edited by Michelene T. H. Chi, Robert Glaser, and M. J. Farr. Lawrence Erlbaum Associates, Hillsdale, NJ.

Logan, Michael H. and Anna R. Dixon. 1994. Agriculture and the Acquisition on Medicinal Plant Knowledge. Pp. 25–45 in *Eating on the Wild Side,* edited by Nina L. Etkin. The University of Arizona Press, Tucson.

Logan, Patrick. 1981. *Irish Country Cures.* Sterling Publishing Company, New York.

Marshall, Howard Wight. 1981. *Folk Architecture in Little Dixie.* The University of Missouri Press, Columbia.

——. 1979. Meat Preservation on the Farm in Missouri's "Little Dixie." *Journal of American Folklore* 92:400–417.

——. 1974. Mr. Westfall's Baskets: Traditional Craftsmanship in Northcentral Missouri. *Mid-South Folklore* 2:43–60.

Martin, Gary J. 1995. *Ethnobotany: A Methods Manual.* Chapman and Hall, London.

McCoy, Edain. 1997. *Mountain Magick: Folk Wisdom from the Heart of Appalachia.* Llewellyn Publications, St. Paul, Minnesota.

McGregory, Jerrilyn. 1997. *Wiregrass Country.* University Press of Mississippi, Jackson.

McNeil, W. K. 1992. Folklore Studies in Arkansas. Pp. 31–56 in *An Arkansas Folklore Sourcebook*, edited by W. K. McNeil and William M. Clements. University of Arkansas Press, Fayetteville.

Medin, Douglas L., Elizabeth B. Lynch, and John D. Coley. 1997. Categorization and Reasoning among Tree Experts: Do all Roads Lead to Rome? *Cognitive Psychology* 32:49–96.

Mitchell, Robert D. 1998. *The Southern Backcountry: A Geographical House Divided.* Pp. 1–35 in The Southern Colonial Backcountry: Interdisciplinary Perspectives on Frontier Communities, edited by David Colin Crass, Steven D. Smith, Martha A. Zierden, and Richard D. Brooks. The University of Tennessee Press, Knoxville.

Moerman, Daniel. 1996. An Analysis of the Food Plants and Drug Plants of Native North America. *Journal of Ethnopharmacology* 52(1)1–22.

——. 1994. North American Food and Drug Plants. Pp. 166–181 in *Eating on the Wild Side*, edited by Nina L. Etkin. The University of Arizona Press, Tucson.

——. 1991. Poisoned Apples and Honeysuckles: The Medicinal Plants of Native America. *Medical Anthropology Quarterly* 3:52–61.

——. 1979. Symbols and Selectivity: A Statistical Analysis of Native American Medical Ethnobotany. *Journal of Ethnopharmacology* 1(2):111–119.

Moerman, Daniel, Robert W. Pemberton, David Kiefer, and Brent Berlin. 1999. A Comparative Analysis of Five Medicinal Floras. *Journal of Ethnobiology* 19(1):49–70.

Mohlenbrock, Robert H. 1986. *Guide to the Vascular Flora of Illinois.* University of Southern Illinois Press, Carbondale.

Nearing, Helen. 1996. Living the Good Life. Pp. 312–320 in *The Ecology of Health: Identifying Issues and Alternatives*, edited by Jennifer Chesworth. Sage Publications, Thousand Oaks, CA.

Nolan, Justin M. 2002. Wild Plant Classification in Little Dixie: Variation in a Regional Culture. *Journal of Ecological Anthropology* 6(1):69–81.

——. 2001. Pursuing the Fruits of Knowledge: Cognitive Ethnobotany in Missouri's Little Dixie. *Journal of Ethnobiology* 21(2):29–51.

——. 1998. The Roots of Tradition: Social Ecology, Cultural Geography, and Medicinal Plant Knowledge in the Ozark-Ouachita Highlands. *Journal of Ethnobiology* 18(2):249–269.

——. 1996. *An Investigation of Medicinal Plant Use and Classification in the Ozark and Ouachita Mountains.* Unpublished Masters Thesis, Department of Anthropology, University of Missouri, Columbia.

Nolan, Justin M. and Michael C. Robbins. 2006. What's Old is New Again: Cultural Change in Hunting and Fishing in Missouri and Arkansas. Pp. 109–27 in *Cultural Analysis and the Navigation of Complexity*, edited by Lisa K. Brandt. University Press of America, Lanham, MD.

———. 2000. Ethnobotany and Ethnicity in the Ozarks: A Reply to Jones. *Human Organization* 59(1):140–142.

———. 1999. Cultural Conservation of Medicinal Plant Use in the Ozarks. *Human Organization* 58(1):67–72.

Nolan, Justin M. and Mary Jo Schneider. 2006. Miracles in the Mountains: Medical Tourism in Rural Arkansas' Ozark Mountains. In *Reimagining Community in a Globalizing World*, edited by Betty Duggan and Steven Folmar. University of Georgia Press, Athens.

Peterson, Lee Allen. 1977. *A Field Guide to Edible Wild Plants: Eastern and Central North America*. Houghton Mifflin, Boston.

Piperno, Dolores and Deborah M. Pearsall. 1998. *The Origins of Agriculture in the Lowland Neotropics*. Academic Press, New York.

Plotkin, Mark J. 1995. The Importance of Ethnobotany for Tropical Forest Conservation. Pp 147–156 in *Ethnobotany: Evolution of a Discipline*, edited by Richard Evans Schultes and Siri von Reis. Dioscordes Press, Portland.

Quinlan, Marsha B. 2005. Considerations for Collecting Freelists in the Field: Examples from Ethnobotany. *Field Methods* 17(3):1–16.

———. 2004. *From the Bush: The Front Line of Health Care in a Caribbean Village*. Wadsworth Publishing, Belmont, CA.

Quinlan, Marsha B., Robert J. Quinlan, and Justin M. Nolan. 2002. Ethnophysiology and Herbal Treatments of Intestinal Worms in a Rural Caribbean Village. *Journal of Ethnopharmacology* 80(1):75–83.

Price, Edward T. 1960. Root Digging in the Appalachians: The Geography of Botanical Drugs. *The Geographical Review* 50:1–20.

Robbins, Michael C. and Justin M. Nolan. 1997. A Measure of Dichotomous Category Bias in Free-Listing Tasks. *Cultural Anthropology Methods Journal* 9(3):8–12.

Romney, A. K. 1999. Culture Consensus as a Statistical Model. *Current Anthropology* 40 (supplement):S103–S115.

Romney, A. K., S. C. Weller, and W. H. Batchelder. 1986. Culture as Consensus: A Theory of Culture and Informant Accuracy. *American Anthropologist* 88(2):313–338.

Rusten, Eric P. and Michael A. Gold. 1995. Indigenous Knowledge Systems and Agroforestry Projects in the Central Hills of Nepal. Pp. 88–111 in *The Cultural Dimension of Development*, edited by D. Michael Warren, L. Jan Slikkerveer, and David Brokensha. Intermediate Technology Publications, London.

Ryan, Gery W., Justin M. Nolan, and Stanley Yoder. 2000. Successive Free-Listing: A New Technique for Generating Explanatory Models. *Field Methods* 12(2):83–107.

Salamon, Sonya. 1995. The Rural People of the Midwest. Pp. 352–366 in *The Changing American Countryside: Rural People and Places, edited by Emery N. Castle.* The University Press of Kansas, Lawrence.

——. 1992. *Prairie Patrimony: Family, Farm, and Community in the Midwest.* University of North Carolina Press, Chapel Hill.

Samson, Fred B. and Fritz L. Knopf. 1996. Preface. Pp. xi–xii in *Prairie Conservation: Preserving North America's Most Endangered Ecosystem*, edited by Fred B. Samson and Fritz L. Knopf. Island Press, Washington D.C.

Schultes, Richard E. 1986. Recognition of Variability in Wild Plants by Indians of the Northwestern Amazon: An Enigma. *Journal of Ethnobiology* 6:229–255.

Schultes, Richard E. and Robert F. Raffauf. 1990. *The Healing Forest: Medicinal and Toxic Plants of Northwest Amazonia.* Dioscordes Press, Portland.

Scott, Shaunna. 1982. Grannies, Mothers, and Babies: An Examination of Traditional Southern Appalachian Midwifery. *Central Issues in Anthropology* 4(2):17–30.

Skillman, Amy E. 1992. No Smoke? No Fire: Contemporary Hamming the Ol' Fashioned Way. Pp. 125–136 in *We Gather Together: Food and Festival in American Life*, edited by Theodore C. Humphrey and Lin T. Humphrey. University of Michigan Research Press, Ann Arbor.

Smith, J. Jerome. 1993. Using ANTHROPAC 3.5 and a Spreadsheet to Compute a Free-List Salience Index. *Cultural Anthropology Methods Newsletter* 5(3):1–3.

Solomon, Gregg. 1997. Conceptual Change and Wine Expertise. *The Journal of the Learning Sciences* 6(1):41–60.

Stepp, John R. 2004. The Role of Weeds as Sources of Pharmaceuticals. *Journal of Ethnopharmacology* 92:163–166.

Steward, Julian. 1955. *Theory and Culture Change.* University of Illinois Press, Urbana.

Thom, R. H. and J. H. Wilson. 1983. The Natural Divisions of Missouri. *Natural Areas Journal* 3(2):44–51.

Trotter, Robert T. 1981. Remedios Caseros: Mexican-American Home Remedies and Community Health Problems. *Social Science and Medicine* 15(2):107–114.

Trotter, Robert T. and Michael H. Logan. 1986. Informant Consensus: A New Approach for Identifying Potentially Effective Medicinal Plants. Pp. 91–112 in *Plants in Indigenous Medicine and Diet: Biobehavioral Approaches*, edited by Nina L. Etkin. Redgrave Publishing, Bedford Hills, New York.

Tuleja, Tad. 1997. Making Ourselves Up: On the Manipulation of Tradition in Small Groups. Pp. 1–23 in *Usable Pasts: Traditions and Groups Expressions in North America*, edited by Tad Tuleja. Utah State University Press, Logan.

Turner, Nancy J. 1988. The Importance of a Rose: Evaluating the Cultural Significance of Plants in Thompson and Lillooet Interior Salish. *American Anthropologist* 90:272–290.

Tyler, Varro E. 1996. "Pharmacognosy"! What's That? You Spell it How? *Economic Botany* 50(1):3–9.

Voeks, R. A. 1996. Tropical Forest Healers and Habitat Preference. *Economic Botany* 50(4):381–400.

Walters, Dirk R. and David J. Keil. 1996. *Vascular Plant Taxonomy* (Fourth edition). Kendall/Hunt Publishing, Dubuque, IA.

Weber, Wallace R. and William T. Corcoran. 1993. *Atlas of Missouri Vascular Plants.* Unpublished manuscript, Southwest Missouri State University.

Weller, Susan C. and A. Kimball Romney. 1988. *Systematic Data Collection*. Sage Publications, Thousand Oaks, CA.

West, James. 1945. *Plainville, USA*. Duell, Sloan, and Pearce. New York, NY.

Wilkinson, Doris Y. 1987. Traditional Medicine in American Families: Reliance on the Wisdom of Elders. *Marriage and Family Review* 11(3–4):65–76.

Wilks, J. H. 1972. *Trees of the British Isles in History and Legend*. Muller, London.

Williams, Michael Ann. 1995. *Great Smoky Mountains Folklife*. University Press of Mississippi, Jackson.

Yatskievych, George. 1999. *Steyermark's Flora of Missouri* (Volume 1). Missouri Department of Conservation, Jefferson City.

Zar, Jerrold H. 1974. *Biostatistical Analysis*. Prentice Hall, Englewood Cliffs, NJ.

Zelinsky, Wilbur. 1992. *The Cultural Geography of the United States* (revised edition). Prentice Hall, Englewood Cliffs, NJ.

Index

applied ethnobotany, 2
ash (*Fraxinus americana*), 11
asparagus (*Asparagus officinalis*), 44
Atlas of Missouri Vascular Plants, 19,
   39

bean family (Fabaceae), 42–43
biodiversity, 77
blackberry (*Rubus spp.*), 21, 49–50, 68
Boone County, Missouri, 6, 15
buckwheat family (Polygonaceae), 44
burdock (*Arcticum minus*), 22–23

Callaway County, Missouri, 15
cattail (*Typha latifolia*), 23
Cherokee Indians, 25–26
Christmas tree, 27
classification. *See* folk classification
Corn belt, 6
cognition, 46, 67–69, 75–76; expert-
   novice differences in, 48, 51–57,
   61–62, 68–74. *See also*
   ethnobotanical cognition
cognitive ethnobotany, 2
cultural consensus: analysis, 69–71;
   model of, 4, 20, 76
cultural conservation, 3, 4, 75
cultural ecology, 1
currant (*Ribes odoratum*), 61

dandelion (*Taraxacum officinale*),
   23–24, 43, 49–50, 68
development. *See* rural development
dill family (Apiaceae), 44

ecology, 59–62; diversity in Missouri,
   39–42
economic botany, 1
emotion, 76
ethnobiological classification, 1, 3, 70
ethnobotanical cognition, 51–52,
   59–62
ethnobotanical classification, 2, 15, 19,
   63–68, 71–74, 76
ethnobotanical evaluation, 55–57
ethnobotany, 1–4; in the United States, 3
experts, 15, 46
expertise, 55

Fayette, Missouri, 6, 12, 35
firewood, 11, 26
flavoring, 35
flour, 28, 30
folk cultures. *See* regional cultures
folk models, 2
folk beliefs, 3–4, 76; Of Great Britain,
   17, 23; Of Ozarks region, 22; Of
   Southern Appalachia, 17, 25. *See*
   also traditional medicine

CPSIA information can be obtained at www.ICGtesting.com
Printed in the USA
LVOW060303260911

247820LV00001B/194/P

9 780761 836537